The Development of God in the Old Testament

CRITICAL STUDIES IN THE HEBREW BIBLE

Edited by

Anselm C. Hagedorn
Universität Osnabrück

Nathan MacDonald
University of Cambridge

Stuart Weeks
Durham University

The Development of God in the Old Testament

Three Case Studies in Biblical Theology

MARKUS WITTE

Translated by Stephen Germany

Winona Lake, Indiana
EISENBRAUNS
2017

Library of Congress Cataloging-in-Publication Data

Names: Witte, Markus, author. | Germany, Stephen translator.
Title: The development of God in the Old Testament : three case studies
  in biblical theology / Markus Witte ; translated by Stephen Germany.
Description: Winona Lake, Indiana : Eisenbrauns, 2017. | Series: Critical
  studies in the Hebrew Bible | Includes bibliographical references and
  index.
Identifiers: LCCN 2017026267 (print) | LCCN 2017027373 (ebook) |
  ISBN 9781575067810 (ePDF) | ISBN 9781575067803 (pbk. : alk.
  paper)
Subjects: LCSH: God (Judaism) | Judaism—History—To 70 A.D. | Bible.
  Old Testament—Criticism, interpretation, etc. | Jesus Christ.
Classification: LCC BM610 (ebook) | LCC BM610 .W58 2017 (print) |
  DDC 296.3/11—dc23
LC record available at https://lccn.loc.gov/2017026267

Contents

Preface

The present volume is a collection of three studies on biblical theology, each of which was originally published in German in different places and in different years (2011, 2012, 2013/2014). Each study has been updated with cross-references to the others for the present collection but otherwise has not been significantly changed. At certain points, references to more recent secondary literature have been incorporated. Each of the three studies can be read on its own, although together they form a thematic unity, as all three revolve around basic questions in the history of the religion of ancient Israel and early Judaism as well as in the theology of the Old Testament. The central subject in each study is the history of God in the Old Testament, and each study aims to demonstrate the traditio-historical, reception-historical, and theological significance of this subject for the discourse on God and Jesus Christ in the New Testament.

I am grateful to the editors of the series *Critical Studies in Hebrew Bible* for the invitation to publish the three studies in this form, particularly my colleague and friend Anselm C. Hagedorn, as well as the publisher, James E. Eisenbraun. I am also grateful to Dr. Stephen Germany for translating the work into English. I thank my staff in the Old Testament Seminar at the Theological Faculty of the Humboldt-Universität zu Berlin, Heye Jensen, Gesine Meier, Brinthanan Puvaneswaran, and Marula Richter, for their assistance in proofreading and in preparing the indexes. Finally, I am indebted to the publishers Hartmut Spenner (Kamen), Mohr Siebeck (Tübingen), and LIT (Münster) for granting permission for the translation and revised publication of the three studies.

This small volume on biblical theology is dedicated to my son, Jason.

Berlin, February 2017
Markus Witte

Acknowledgments

Chapter 1. From El Shaddai to Pantokrator: Reflections on the History of Israelite and Jewish Religion and on Biblical Theology through the Lens of a Divine Name.

Revised and augmented version of:

"Vom EL SCHADDAJ zum PANTOKRATOR – Ein Überblick zur israelitisch-jüdischen Religionsgeschichte," Pp. 211–56 in *Studien zur Hebräischen Bibel und ihrer Nachgeschichte. Beiträge der 32. Internationalen Ökumenischen Konferenz der Hebräischlehrenden, Frankfurt a.M. 2009.* Edited by Johannes F. Diehl and Markus Witte. Kleine Untersuchungen zur Sprache des Alten Testaments und seiner Umwelt 12.13. Kamen: Hartmut Spenner, 2011.

Chapter 2. From Divine Justice to Human Justice.

Revised and augmented version of:

"Von der Gerechtigkeit Gottes und des Menschen im Alten Testament," Pp. 91–127 in *Gerechtigkeit. Themen der Theologie 6.* Edited by Markus Witte. UTB 3662. Tübingen: Mohr Siebeck, 2012.

Chapter 3. From Yahweh to the Messiah: Images of God in the Old Testament as Background for the Discourse on Jesus Christ in the New Testament.

Revised and augmented version of:

Jesus Christus im Alten Testament. Eine biblisch-theologische Skizze. Salzburger Exegetische Theologische Vorträge 4. Münster: LIT, 2013.
"Jesus Christus im Spiegel des Alten Testaments," Pp. 13–70 in *Jesus Christus. Themen der Theologie 9.* Edited by Jens Schröter. UTB 4213. Tübingen: Mohr Siebeck, 2014.

I warmly thank the publishing houses *Hartmut Spenner* (Kamen), *LIT* (Münster) and *Mohr Siebeck* (Tübingen) for their kind permission to reprint the original publications in a translated and augmented version. A note on citations: The abbreviations for biblical and extrabiblical sources as well as for secondary literature follow the SBL Handbook of Style. In the footnotes, only the last name of the author, an abbreviated form of the title, and the page number are provided. The bibliography at the end of the volume includes all works cited as well as further relevant literature.

Unless otherwise noted, biblical quotations are from the New Revised Standard Version (1989).

Introduction

Old Testament theology—the presentation of the discourse on God in the Old Testament in its different literary, historical, and systematic contexts—is a significant component of Christian biblical theology. I use the term "biblical theology" to denote a literary and historical presentation of the discourse on and to God in the Old and New Testaments with respect to their fundamental significance for understanding human existence before God. Accordingly, biblical theology is a theology that sheds light on human existence on the basis of both the Old and New Testaments.[1]

In the first three centuries CE, Christianity developed from different strands of Judaism. It preserved the sacred scriptures of Israel as an interpretation of the life, death, and resurrection of Jesus and as a source of meaning and structure in the lives of individual Christians. Consequently, the discourse on God in these scriptures constitutes both the heritage and the subject of biblical theology. Schleiermacher argued that the Old Testament's sole purpose was for legitimating Christian tradition and cultic practice.[2] But the importance of the Old Testament in the church is by no means limited to its quotation in certain New Testament passages or

---

1. On the many forms of biblical theology, see Kraus, *Die Biblische Theologie*; Reventlow, *Hauptprobleme der Biblischen Theologie*; Oeming, *Gesamtbiblische Theologien*; Childs, *Theology*; Janowski, "Biblische Theologie"; idem, *Theologie und Exegese des Alten Testaments*; Moberly, *Old Testament Theology*; and the *Jahrbuch für Biblische Theologie* (published since 1986); for an example of its application, see Feldmeier and Spieckermann, *Der Gott der Lebendigen*.

2. Schleiermacher, *Der christliche Glaube*, cited here from the unrevised third edition from 1836, vol. 2, p. 346: "Die alttestamentischen Schriften verdanken ihre Stelle in unserer Bibel theils den Berufungen der neutestamentischen auf sie, theils dem geschichtlichen Zusammenhang des christlichen Gottesdienstes mit der jüdischen Synaogoge, ohne daß sie deshalb die normale Dignität oder die Eingebung der neutestamentischen theilen." This passage and the material that followed it are not present in the first edition from 1820/1821 and can be understood as an explicit differentiation between the Old and New Testaments, culminating in Schleiermacher's suggestion that, in light of its traditio-historical significance, the Old Testament should not be abandoned by the Church but should nevertheless be regarded as subordinate to the New Testament with respect to its character as divine revelation and should continue to stand alongside the New Testament for purely practical reasons, "da die jezige Stellung nicht undeutlich die Forderung aufstellt, daß man sich erst durch das ganze A.T. durcharbeiten müsse, um auf richtigem Wege zum neuen zu gelangen" (p. 351). On this, see Smend, "Schleiermachers Kritik," 128–44.

its use in worship. Rather, it is based on the conviction—gained from the perspective of faith in Jesus Christ—of the identity of the actions of God. As creator God gives meaning to life, as judge he provide and enforces protective laws, and as redeemer he provides a deep communion that overcomes suffering and death for those who trust in him.

Even though the broader point of reference of Old Testament theology is the New Testament and its primary functional context is the Church, the Old Testament's statements about God should be considered in light of their own history and meaning. Anything else would be a step backward in three respects: first, from the differentiation between exegesis and dogmatics that emerged during the eighteenth century; second, from the religio-historical approach established in Old Testament research during the nineteenth century; and third, from the renewed recognition in Christianity of the texts in the Old Testament as the sacred scripture of Judaism or as "Israel's Bible" during the second half of the twentieth century.

The contribution of Old Testament theology to biblical theology cannot be restricted to presenting the origins and contents of selected Old Testament texts that were either of particular significance to the New Testament authors or that played an important role in the formation of the Churches' teachings. Rather, the task of Old Testament theology as a part of (and not as an aspect or a form of)[3] biblical theology is to clarify the overall theological structure of the Old Testament as part of the Christian Bible.[4] This involves describing the theology of individual books, individual blocks of tradition, and individual texts.[5] In this respect, the presentation of the theology (or more precisely, the theologies) of, for example, the book of Job, the primeval history in Genesis 1–9 (sic!),[6] or the Priestly Writing in the Pentateuch is as theologically justified as the presentation of the theology of the Gospel of Matthew, the Q source, or the pre-Markan Passion narrative.

The textual basis of Old Testament theology consists of both the Hebrew and Greek versions of the sacred scriptures of early Judaism. In light

---

3. Thus, however, Barr, *Concept.*
4. On this see, for example, Rendtorff, *Theologie des Alten Testaments,* vol. 2, pp. 280–317; Moberly, *Old Testament Theology,* 1–4.
5. Cf. Schmitt, "Die Einheit der Schrift," 326–45.
6. The biblical primeval history is usually identified in Gen 1–11, although the conceptual arc of "creation—questioning of creation through a flood—reordering of creation after the flood," which is also found in ancient Near Eastern myths of human origins (cf., for example, the Akkadian "Epic of Atra-ḫasis," *COS* 1.130:450–53; *TUAT* 3:612–45; *TUAT NF* 8:132–43), suggests that the primeval history should be restricted to Gen 1:1–9:29 (cf. Witte, *Die biblische Urgeschichte,* 48–51).

of the textual history reflected by the manuscript evidence, the Hebrew textual forms cannot simply be equated with the Masoretic Text, nor the Greek textual forms with the Septuagint. This is the case even though the major codices of the Masoretic Text and the Septuagint, with all their micro- and macrotextual differences, represent the primary points of reference for both dogmatic and pragmatic reasons. Old Testament theology must take into account the different linguistic forms as well as the diverse materials and compositional characteristics of the sacred scriptures of early Judaism. In terms of the history of the canon, the Septuagint represents the actual Old Testament. The consideration of the Masoretic Text stems from several factors: first, in terms of textual history, the Masoretic Text (or another Hebrew text that preceded it) served as the *Vorlage* for the translation of the Septuagint; second, in terms of reception history, the Bible that Jesus knew was a Hebrew text; and third, from an ecumenical perspective, the Masoretic Text has been the authoritative text in Judaism since late antiquity. Regarding the contribution of Old Testament theology to biblical theology, this means that the theology of the Old Testament in both its Hebrew and Greek forms must be emphasized. Moreover, the transformations that resulted from the translation of individual Hebrew terms and motifs into Greek, which also reflect the Hellenistic Greek conceptual world, need to be highlighted. Finally, the theology of the books that were only transmitted in the Greek canon of the Septuagint (despite their Jewish origins) must also be taken into consideration, as these played a significant role in New Testament Christology and ethics as well as in the formation of early Church doctrine.[7]

The first study in this volume, "From El Shaddai to Pantokrator," traces key aspects in the development of the understanding of God in the Old Testament through the Hebrew divine title שדי אל and one of its most important Greek equivalents, παντοκράτωρ. The use of the divine title אל שדי in the Hebrew Bible, its ancient Near Eastern religious background, its transferral into Hellenistic Judaism, and its theological significance reveal fundamental aspects of a biblical theology that is equally indebted to comparative philology and to the history of religion.

Following this diachronic example of a biblical theology, the essay "From Divine Justice to Human Justice" is a more synchronically oriented thematic study. In addition to providing an overview of the concepts involved and their tradition history, this essay discusses justice as a central theme of the theology of the Old Testament and as a fundamental category

---

7. See, for example, Sirach 24, Wisdom 7, Baruch 3–4 in connection to Christology, or Tobit 4 in connection to New Testament ethics.

in defining the relationship between God and humanity. This tracing of
the theological understanding of justice spans the primeval history to the
Wisdom of Solomon by way of the David narratives, the prophetic literature (with the book of Habakkuk as a case study), and the book of Job.
It concludes with a sketch of Old Testament theology relating to law and
justice as a form of philological, historical, aesthetic, and applied inquiry.
This broader outlook leads into the third and most detailed case study on
the representation of images of God in the Old Testament as background
to the discourse on Jesus Christ in the New Testament.

On the one hand, the title "From Yahweh to the Messiah" alludes
to the approach of the first essay, which presents theology as a form of
religio-historical onomastics. On the other hand, corresponding to the
second essay, it reflects the traditio-historical presentation of images of
God in the Old Testament as a basis for the New Testament's discourse on
Jesus Christ. In other words, the ways of speaking and thinking about God
in the Old Testament constitute the religio-historical and theological basis
for the discourse on God's acts in the person of Jesus Christ in the New
Testament. In this respect, the theology of the Old Testament and that of
the New Testament are inseparably connected, even if discrete theologies
of the Old and New Testaments can be identified.

The approach to biblical theology in all three essays in the volume, but
especially in the third essay, is based on traditio-historical and structural
models from the last third of the twentieth century,[8] which are complemented here by a literary-historical approach. In all of these approaches,
teleological reductionism must be avoided, given that the literary and
traditio-historical relationships among the scriptures of ancient Israel that
later became the Old Testament are much more complex than what was
assumed in the 1970s. Consistent attention to the texts from Qumran and
to Jewish literature from the Hellenistic and Roman periods, texts that did
not become part of the biblical canon, reveals the plurality of the religio-
historical milieu in which the New Testament's discourse on Jesus Christ
developed. In addition, Jewish-Christian dialogue during the past several
decades indicates that the New Testament's reading of Israel's scriptures is
a possible, but not the only, form of using and understanding those scriptures. Here, a foundational observation by Georg Fohrer (1915–2002)
can be mentioned:

> In the end, the Old Testament is not like a room that has only
> one door that opens onto the New Testament. It has many doors

---

8. Cf. Preuß, *Das Alte Testament*, 120–140; Gese, "Erwägungen zur Einheit," 11–30.

and is open on many sides. The Qumran community interpreted the Old Testament scriptures in terms of its own history and regarded itself as the true Israel. Apocalyptic piety based itself on the Old Testament, and Rabbi Akiva recognized Bar Kokhba as the promised messiah and regarded him as the promised star from Num 24:17. Rabbinic piety also emphasized obedience to the Old Testament, and the piety attested in the writings of Philo (despite their assumed Hellenistic religious influence) also rests on the Old Testament. In the same way, the early Christian community and, later, Islam likewise invoked the Old Testament. Thus, the Old Testament need not lead to the New Testament and is not open to the New Testament in any simple way.[9]

Of course, in the context of Christian theology, the sacred scriptures of early Judaism (in varying scope) became the "Old Testament" through Christology, and from a Christian perspective the New Testament is where the Old Testament is fulfilled—not the other way around, as the title of Frank Crüsemann's book *Das Alte Testament als Wahrheitsraum des Neuen: Die neue Sicht der christlichen Bibel* (2011) might suggest. Yet, the literature of Israel collected in the Old Testament also took on its own Jewish shaping in the form of the Hebrew Bible or Tanakh and continues to generate new interpretations today. In this way, the concept of the "dual reception" ("*zweifache Nachgeschichte*") of the writings of ancient Israel and Judah, developed largely by Rolf Rendtorff (1925–2014), has lasting meaning.[10] Thus, it is a question of particular strands in the diverse theologies in the Old Testament that were selected and expanded upon from the perspective of faith in Jesus Christ, not a question of a *single* strand or a *single* theology. It is precisely the factors of diversity and selection that are of significance for the history of biblical literature and tradition. It is always only certain developments and themes that are taken

---

9. "Schließlich ist das Alte Testament nicht wie ein Zimmer, das nur eine Tür hat, die sich in den Raum des Neuen Testaments öffnet. Es hat viele Türen und ist nach vielen Seiten offen. Die Gemeinde von Qumran hat die alttestamentlichen Schriften auf ihre eigene Geschichte hin ausgelegt und sich selbst für das wahre Israel gehalten. Die apokalyptische Frömmigkeit berief sich auf das Alte Testament, und der Rabbi Aqiba hat Bar Kochba als den verheißenen Messias anerkannt und den verheißenen Stern von Num 24,17 auf ihn gedeutet. Auch die rabbinische Frömmigkeit lebte vom Gehorsam gegen das Alte Testament, und die in den Schriften Philos bezeugte Frömmigkeit ruhte bei aller angenommenen hellenistischen Bildungsreligion ebenfalls auf dem Alten Testament. Genauso berief sich die frühe christliche Gemeinde auf es und später der Islam. So muß das Alte Testament durchaus nicht zum Neuen Testament führen und ist nicht einfach dorthin offen" (Fohrer, "Das Alte Testament," 294); similarly Brueggemann, *Theology*, 729–33.

10. On this see the overview in Rendtorff, *Theologie des Alten Testaments*, 304–5.

from prior tradition, expanded upon literarily, and reinterpreted. Selection and variability characterizes inner-biblical references to earlier texts, the earliest extrabiblical history of reception (as can be seen in the frequent reference to texts from Deuteronomy, the Psalms, and the book of Isaiah in the literature from Qumran as well as in the New Testament), and the distinct forms of the canon in Judaism and in the different Christian denominations.

It is especially in the third essay in this volume that selected Old Testament themes found in the New Testament's discourse on Jesus Christ will be discussed in terms of their literary and religio-historical development.[11] In doing so, significant structures, motifs, and traditions in the Old Testament's discourse on God will be shown to be the point of departure and the background for the New Testament's presentation of God's actions in the person of Jesus Christ. Moreover, all three case studies will address to what extent the theologies of the Old Testament can be applied to the New Testament and can serve as the basis for a biblical theology.

---

11. For such a selective approach, see also Moberly, *Old Testament Theology.*

CHAPTER I

From El Shaddai to Pantokrator:

Reflections on the History of Israelite and Jewish Religion and on Biblical Theology through the Lens of a Divine Name

> for some call him 'Zeus' (Ζῆνα), and others 'Dia' (Δία); but the two in combination express the nature of the god, which is just what we said a name should be able to do.[1]

Names are like a mirror: they reveal something about the nature, function, and context of the thing that they describe. Correspondingly, divine names reflect the nature, function, and background of the god called by that name.[2] Divine names are thus also a mirror of religions in their historical and cultural contexts. From a literary perspective, divine names are the unifying thread of sacred scripture. Moreover, the enduring use of a particular divine name reveals the theological self-understanding of a particular community of faith.

1. El Shaddai (אל שדי)

1.1. The Textual Evidence in the Hebrew Bible

The divine name שדי occurs 48 times in the Hebrew Bible: 8 times in the composite form אל שדי (the "long form") and 40 times as the absolute form שדי (the "short form"). The combination with the general Semitic

---

1. Plato, *Crat.* 396a, trans. Harold N. Fowler ("Cratylus," 48–49).
2. On this, see also Zimmermann, *Die Namen des Vaters*, 7–20, and Hartenstein, "Die Geschichte JHWHs," 73–95, who refers in particular to the relationship between the names of God in the Old Testament and the name Yahweh.

word אֵל for God indicates that שַׁדַּי—at least in the Hebrew Bible—is, like the word עֶלְיוֹן ("Most High"), an epithet that can also be used as an independent divine name.[3]

These occurrences are concentrated in two blocks of text: the passages assigned to the Priestly Writing in Gen 17:1, 28:3, 35:11, 43:14, 48:3, and Exod 6:3 and the poetic portions of the book of Job. In the latter, with only one exception (Job 6:14), the absolute form שַׁדַּי always occurs in parallelism with another divine name (אֱלוֹהַּ, אֱלֹהִים, אֵל).[4] In addition, there are two occurrences in the Psalms (Ps 68:15, 91:1), the book of Ruth (1:20–21), the Balaam oracles (Num 24:4, 16), and the book of Ezekiel (1:24, 10:5) and one occurrence each in Gen 49:25, Isa 13:6, and Joel 1:15. Without exception, אֵל שַׁדַּי / שַׁדַּי appears in direct speech, whether in prayers or in revelatory speeches by or about God. Finally, three personal names containing the element שַׁדַּי appear in Priestly or post-Priestly lists.[5]

1.2. The Literary-Historical Place of the Attestations

(a) I will take the Priestly occurrences of שַׁדַּי as a starting point for the literary-historical classification of the term, since here (1) the term *El Šaddai* is used in a specific way and (2) there is a broad scholarly consensus that the Priestly Writing dates to the sixth or fifth century BCE. In the Priestly Writing, אֵל שַׁדַּי serves as a divine name during the ancestral age, which is preceded by the age when humanity experiences God as אֱלֹהִים and is followed by the age of Israel, which encounters God as יהוה via Moses. Thus, the revelation of Yahweh's name in Exod 6:2–3 connects directly to Yahweh's self-revelation to Abraham under the name אֵל שַׁדַּי in Gen 17:1. The Priestly chain of the references to אֵל שַׁדַּי is closely tied to the motifs of "blessing," "increase," and "fruitfulness."

(b) The use of שַׁדַּי in the Joseph oracle (Gen 49:22–26) presupposes the Priestly blessing over Joseph in Gen 48:3–4:

---

3. The boundary between divine names, epithets, and attributes can be fluid; on this problem, see also Hartenstein, "Die Geschichte JHWHs," 94; for a systematic survey and classification of divine names and epithets in the ancient Near East, see Uehlinger, "Arbeit an altorientalischen Gottesnamen," 23–71.

4. Job 19:29 (שַׁדִין, Ketib שַׁדִּין, Qere שַׁדּוּן) is not a further attestation of שַׁדַּי but rather a combination of the relative particle שֶׁ / שַׁ with the noun דִּין "judgment" (for a discussion, see Cheney, *Dust, Wind, and Agony*, 238–39; Clines, *Job 1–20*, 435).

5. עַמִּישַׁדַּי ("my kinsman [= guardian] is Šaddai," Num 1:12, 2:25, 7:66, 71, 10:25; on this see also p. 17 n. 53); צוּרִישַׁדַּי ("my rock is Šaddai," Num 1:6, 2:12, 7:36, 41, 10:19, cf. Σαρασαδαι [*v.l.* Σαλασαδαι, Σαρισαδαι] in Jdt 8:1); and probably שַׁדֵיאוּר ("Šaddai is light," Num 1:5, 2:10, 7:30, 35, 10:18).

> By the God of your father who will help you, and by[6] שׁדי who
> will bless you,
> With blessings of heaven above, blessings of the deep that lies
> beneath,
> Blessings of the breasts (שׁדים) and of the womb. (Gen 49:25)

Gen 49:25 (together with vv. 24b and 26) represents a secondary addition
that is partially derived from Deut 33:13–17, providing an inner-biblical
etymology associated with the Hebrew word שׁד "breast."

(c) Within the third and fourth Balaam oracles, שׁדי stands in parallelism with the divine names אל and עליון (Num 24:4, 16):

> The oracle of one who hears the words of אל {and knows the
> knowledge of עליון},[7]
> who sees the vision of שׁדי, who falls down, but with eyes
> uncovered.

In terms of their literary history, the third and fourth Balaam oracles—like
the most basic compositional layer of the Balaam pericope in Numbers
22–24—belong to a post-Priestly stage of composition,[8] even if their parallels with the Transjordanian Deir ʿAlla Inscription (*KAI* 312), which
possibly dates to the ninth or eighth century BCE, point to an older history of tradition.[9] The frequency of the divine names אל, עליון, and שׁדי
in Num 24:4, 16 highlights the importance of the blessing that Balaam
utters over "Israel." This creates a compositional arc with the blessing that
Abraham receives in the name of אל עליון from the priest-king Melchizedek of Salem (Gen 14:19) and with the blessing that Abraham himself
receives from אל שׁדי (Gen 17:1).

(d) In the poetry of the book of Job, שׁדי combined with the terms
אל, אלוה, and אלהים serves as a substitute for the name of Yahweh, which
is not used by figures who are described as non-Israelites: Job, Eliphaz the
Temanite, Bildad the Shuhite, Zophar the Naamathite, and Elihu.[10] Here,
a semantic difference between אל, אלוה, אלהים, and שׁדי is not discern-
ible (see, for example, the similar phrasing of Job 4:9 [נשׁמת אלוה], 32:8

---

6. וְאֵת is often emended to וְאֵל ("and [by] El"), although this is unnecessary (thus
with Seebass, *Genesis III*, 166).

7. This colon is only found in 24:16aβ and should possibly be added to 24:4.

8. Witte, "Der Segen Bileams," 191–213.

9. Cf. Blum, "Kombination I"; idem, "Schreibkunst"; *TUAT* 2:138–47; Jaroš, *Inschriften des Heiligen Landes*, no. 195; *COS* 2.27:140–45.

10. The only occurrence of the tetragrammaton in the poetry of Job—with the exception of the superscriptions in 38:1, 40:1, 3, 6, and 42:1—in Job 12:9 is secondary and
possibly a quotation from Isa 41:20.

[נִשְׁמַת־שַׁדַּי], and 37:10 [נִשְׁמַת־אֵל]).[11] It is possible that there are poetic reasons for the change in the archaizing divine names. It is striking, however, that (1) the occurrences of שַׁדַּי are more frequent in the second half of the book; (2) within the poetry, שַׁדַּי is the last explicit divine name placed in Job's mouth (6:4, 31:35); and (3) שַׁדַּי appears in the very short second(!) speech by Yahweh in 40:2, in direct reference to Job 31:35.[12]

The poetry of Job originated around the same time as the Priestly Writing. If one considers further parallels between the Priestly Writing and the poetry of Job, such as the conceptions of creation in Gen 1 and Job 38–39, then it cannot be ruled out that the Joban poet knew the Priestly Writing's three-stage concept of revelation (יהוה—אֵל שַׁדַּי—אֱלֹהִים)[13] and thus allowed Job and his friends to refer to God as אֵל, אֱלוֹהַּ, אֱלֹהִים, or שַׁדַּי and only used the tetragrammaton in the superscription of the divine speech(es), even though for him—as for the Priestly Writing—אֵל, אֱלוֹהַּ, אֱלֹהִים, or שַׁדַּי are ultimately synonyms for Yahweh. From the perspective of the literarily later narrative framework and the epilogue in the Septuagint version of Job (Job 42:17 LXX), which describes Job (under the alias Jobab) as "the fifth after Abraham," the use of the divine name שַׁדַּי by contemporaries of Israel's ancestors is quite understandable.

(e) The double use of שַׁדַּי in Ruth 1:20–21 stands out within the book of Ruth, which otherwise uses the divine name Yahweh, even in direct speech. In contrast, in Ruth 1:20–21—as in Gen 49:25 and Num 24:4, 16—שַׁדַּי occurs in a poetic verse which is also a quote from Job 27:2:[14]

> [20] She said to them, "Call me no longer Naomi ["Graceful"], call me Mara ["Bitter"], for שַׁדַּי has dealt bitterly with me. [21] I went away full, but יהוה has brought me back empty; why call me Naomi when יהוה has dealt harshly with me, and שַׁדַּי has brought calamity upon me?"

11. Thus with Lévêque, *Job et son dieu*, I, 173–79, against Cheney, *Dust, Wind, and Agony*, 239–40.

12. Could this be an indication that this divine speech is more original than the two longer speeches in Job 38:1–39:30 and 40:6–41:26?

13. Within this context, Ziemer, *Abram – Abraham*, 329 offers an idiosyncratic explanation of the use of אֵל שַׁדַּי in terms of the theory of Gematria, assigning the three-stage concept of revelation to a "final compositional layer" of the Pentateuch: thus, the numerical value of אֵל שַׁדַּי (345) corresponds with the letters of the name of Moses (מֹשֶׁה).

14. Cf. Job 3:20, 7:11, 10:1, 23:2, as well as Job 30:11 and 37:23, with Ruth 1:20–21. For the notion that Ruth 1:20 quotes Job 27:2, see already Siegfried and Stade, *Hebräisches Wörterbuch*, 778.

Through the use of the divine name שׁדי, the poet styles Naomi as Job's sister, just as he will later characterize Ruth as Leah's and Rachel's sister (Ruth 4:11).

(f) Isa 13:6 is part of a proto-apocalyptic "Day-of-Yahweh Text," which presupposes the capture of Babylon by the Persian king Cyrus II in 539 BCE. This single occurrence of שׁדי in the book of Isaiah reveals that 13:6 is an isolated addition that forms a play on words between שׁדי and the Hebrew verb שׁדד "to be violent" or the Hebrew noun שׁד "destruction":

Wail, for the day of *Yahweh* is near;
it will come like violence (כשׁד) from *the violent one* (משׁדי).[15]

Thus, in older Hebrew philology, שׁדי was sometimes derived etymologically from שׁדד, and the suffixed -*y* was explained as a plural marker or as an analogy to אדני.[16]

Joel 1:15 cites Isa 13:6 and thus cannot be a pre-Priestly attestation of שׁדי.[17]

(g) The same applies for the two occurrences of שׁדי in the book of Ezekiel.

Ezek 1:24:
When they moved, I heard the sound of their wings like the sound of mighty waters, like the thunder of שׁדי, a sound of tumult like the sound of an army; when they stopped, they let down their wings (cf. Rev 19:6).

Ezek 10:5:
The sound of the wings of the cherubim was heard as far as the outer court, like the voice of אל שׁדי when he speaks.

---

15. The LXX does not reflect this play on words, since it translates שׁד with συντριβή and שׁדי with θεός (καὶ συντριβὴ παρὰ τοῦ θεοῦ ἥξει "and destruction will come from the Lord").

16. Gesenius, *Thesaurus philologicus criticus*, III, 1366–67; Levy, *Chaldäisches Wörterbuch über die Targumim*, s.v.; Siegfried and Stade, *Hebräisches Wörterbuch*, 778; König, *Hebräisches und aramäisches Wörterbuch*, 485; Noth, *Die israelitischen Personennamen*, 130–31; Zorell, *Lexicon Hebraicum*, 823. On the play on words, see also Isa 13:4, where the divine title יהוה צבאות ("Yahweh [the god] of the armies," philologically acceptable) is combined with the word צבא "army."

17. In contrast to Isa 13:6 LXX, here the LXX mimics the play on words כשׁד משׁדי, although it remains an open question whether the LXX itself "neutralized" שׁדי or whether it found שׁד in its *Vorlage* (cf. שׁדד in v. 10) (καὶ ὡς ταλαιπωρία ἐκ ταλαιπωρίας ἥξει "and it will come as trouble upon trouble").

Here, the exceptional use of שׁדי and the literary-critical analysis of both verses indicate that these verses are additions. That these additions are apparently very late is confirmed by the Septuagint, which in Ezek 1:24 originally did not have an equivalent for שׁדי [18] and in Ezek 10:5 transcribes שׁדי with the *hapax* Σαδδαι. [19]

(h) Two occurrences in the Psalms remain to be discussed. Psalm 68, often regarded in earlier scholarship as very old, was shown by Henrik Pfeiffer (2005) to be a literarily composite poem from the Hellenistic period. The most basic material in the psalm, to which Pfeiffer assigns v. 15, draws on the "history of salvation" as presented in the Pentateuch. [20] Thus, the use of שׁדי in Ps 68:15—if it is even original here—should be evaluated as post-Priestly:

When ישׁדי scattered kings there, snow fell on Zalmon. [21]

The second occurrence in the Psalms, Ps 91:1, is found in a series of divine titles (vv. 1–3: הוא אלהים, יהוה, עליון) within a postexilic song of trust describing the suppliant's expectations of God as his all-embracing protector: [22]

> You who live in the shelter of עליון, who abide in the shadow of שׁדי,
> will say to יהוה, "My refuge and my fortress; my God, in whom I trust."
> For he will deliver you from the snare of the fowler and from the deadly pestilence.

(i) In the Qumran writings, שׁדי is thus far attested only five times. 4Q175, 11 is a quotation of Num 24:16, and 11Q11 VI, 3 is a quotation of Psalm 91. Beyond the biblical quotations, 4Q252 III, 12 contains a

---

18. It is only in later variants and in the translations of Symmachus, Theodotion, and Aquila that different equivalents such as ἱκανός, θεὸς σαδδαι, σαδδαικανος / σαδαι ἱκανος are found; on this, see §2 below.

19. For the transcription Σαδδαι see also some of the church fathers (Eusebius, *Dem. ev.* 10.8.28–30, Epiphanius, *Pan.* 2.86.8, Origen, *Mart.* 46.14); here, too, ἱκανός appears in some variants as well as among later Greek translators.

20. Exodus and wilderness journey (vv. 8–11), conquest (vv. 12–15), arrival at Zion (vv. 16–19). The precise point of reference of v. 15 is unclear (Num 24:3, 7–8, 16?); cf. Pfeiffer, *Jahwes Kommen*, 204–57.

21. There are countless conjectures regarding this verse; it possibly reflects a theophany motif expressing the interplay of Yahweh's celestial and terrestrial actions (cf. Job 38:22–23); cf. Brown, *Israel and Hellas III*, 68–69.

22. On this, see also Hartenstein, "Die Geschichte JHWHs," 89.

request for blessing in the name of שׁדי אל, and 4Q511 8, 6 (and probably also frag. 116 3) employs שׁדי in assurances of divine protection as in Psalm 91. In this respect, 11Q11 and 4Q511 are early attestations of the use of the divine epithet שׁדי in magical texts serving to ward off demons.

(j) To summarize the foregoing literary-historical overview: Within the Hebrew Bible, there are no occurrences of שׁדי אל or שׁדי that can be securely evaluated as pre-Priestly. All biblical occurrences of the term outside the Priestly Writing could be literarily dependent on the latter. This means that the Priestly Writing presumably introduced the divine designation שׁדי into the Hebrew Bible in the long form אל שׁדי, which was later able to stand alone in the short form שׁדי.[23] This usage is a further example of the innovative nature of the Priestly Writing, which, as is well known, can also be seen in its coining of the technical term ברא ("to create," exclusively with "God" as its subject) to describe the Priestly theology of creation or in the linking of the primeval history, the ancestral narratives, and the exodus narrative for the first time.[24]

Nevertheless, the question remains whether the Priestly Writing developed the name שׁדי itself or whether it drew on an ancient Near Eastern divine name.[25] In any event, the limited number of occurrences in the Psalms and the absence of the term in the Elephantine Papyri, in which elements that preceded and existed alongside Yahwism in Israelite-Judean religion persisted, speak against the assumption that שׁדי is a very old divine name.

1.3. The Religio-Historical Dimension

The religio-historical dimension relates to two aspects that are closely connected: (1) the etymology of שׁדי and its relationship to a particular linguistic and cultural milieu, and (2) the reconstruction of a form of ancient Israelite religion that preceded and/or existed alongside Yahwism based on the etymology of the term or on a traditio-historical analysis of its biblical attestations.

(a) The connection between the Hebrew term שׁדי and the Akkadian word *šadû / šaddû* "mountain" goes back to the time of the systematic

---

23. On this, see already Köhler, *Theologie des Alten Testaments*, 28–29; Görg, "Šaddaj," 13–15; Knauf, "El Šaddaj," 22–26, as well as the detailed discussion in Steins, שׁדי, 1083–1104.

24. On this, see de Pury, "Gott," 133; Schmid, *Erzväter und Exodus*; Gertz, *Tradition und Redaktion*.

25. Thus, most recently, Hartenstein, "Die Geschichte JHWHs," 84–85, who speaks of an "old divine name" without a more precise identification.

mining of cuneiform literature at the end of the nineteenth century.[26] The word *šadû* can be used as an epithet for different deities and emphasizes the powerful and protective character of the deity (cf., e.g., the reference to the god Enlil as *šadû rabû* "great mountain").[27] Like the derivation of the word *šaddû'a* "mountain dweller" from *šadû*, אל שדי can thus be interpreted as "El / God who comes from the mountain,"[28] whereby the ending -*ay* is understood as a northwest Semitic gentilic suffix.[29]

This explanation fits well with the religio-historical typology of Yahweh as a mountain- and storm-god.[30] It finds a thematic counterpoint in the biblical references to Yahweh as "my rock" (צורי, cf. Deut 18:3).[31] Following this theory, the Priestly Writing would have integrated an Akkadian divine epithet (as an archaism?) into its own theology.

(b) With reference to the connection of a divine title with the word *šd* "field" (cf. *ʿttrt šd* "Astarte of the Field"[32] and *il šdj* "El of the Field"[33]), Manfred Weippert (1961) and Oswald Loretz (1980) have suggested a derivation of אל שדי from an original reading אל שדה "God of the Field."[34] Although in 1975 Weippert abandoned this interpretation in favor of the Akkadian derivation discussed above, it was taken up again by Ernst Axel Knauf in 1999. In doing so, Knauf built upon the religio-historical hypothesis that אל שדי / אל שדה reflects the "Lord of the Wilderness" or the "Lord of the Animals" who was revered in Syria–Palestine during the Iron Age.[35] This theory was formulated even more pointedly by Bernhard Lang (2001): "A special Hebrew name for the Lord of the Animals could have been Shaddai or El-Shaddai."[36] Thus, according to Lang, corresponding

---

26. Friedrich Delitzsch, *Prolegomena*, 95–96; Zimmern and Winckler, *Die Keilinschriften*, 358; on the problem of the "s"-sound in Akk. *šadû* and Heb. שדי and the doubling of the "d," see the detailed discussions by Cross, *Canaanite Myth*, 52–60 and Weippert, "שַׁדַּי Šaddaj," 877–81.

27. *TUAT* 2:35.33; 2:187.328; 2:656.57; *COS* 1.163:531.11; 1.183:585.21; 1.183: 588.18.

28. Albright, "The Names *SHADDAI*," 184–85.

29. *HAL* 4:1320; Lévêque, *Job et son dieu*, I, 163–68; Cross, *Canaanite Myth*, 55; Weippert, "שַׁדַּי Šaddaj," 878–79.

30. Cf. 1 Kgs 20:23, 28.

31. Cf. Deut 32:31, 37; Ps 18:47, 19:15, 28:1, 31:3, 62:3, 7, 71:3, 92:16, 144:1; Hab 1:12.

32. Cf. the list in *KTU*² 4.182:55, 58.

33. Cf. the short hymn in *KTU*² 1.108,12 (*il.šd.jsd*). In the expression *bʿl šd* in a list of names (*KTU*² 4.183), the word *bʿl* probably means "owner."

34. Weippert, "Erwägungen zur Etymologie," 42–62; Loretz, "Der kanaanäische Ursprung," 420–21; cf. Wifall, "El Shaddai," 24–32.

35. Knauf, "SHADDAY," 749–53.

36. "Eine spezielle hebr. Bezeichnung für den H(errn) d(er) T(iere) dürfte Schaddai respektive El-Schaddai gewesen sein" (Lang, "Herr der Tiere," 862–63; idem, *Jahwe*, 131).

a.   b.   c.

Fig. 1. (a) Lord of the Animals between two ostriches, decoration on a stamp seal from Beth Shemesh, 10th/9th century BCE; (b) Lord of the Animals between two ostriches, decoration on a stamp seal from Tell en-Naṣbeh, 10th/9th century BCE; (c) Lord of the animals between two ibexes, decoration on a scarab, 12th/11th centuries BCE. From Keel and Uehlinger, *Altorientalische Miniaturkunst*, p. 22, fig. 12.

images on seal impressions should be regarded as visual representations of שׁדי אל (cf. fig. 1 a–c).

There are at least two problematic aspects of this interpretation. First, the translation of *šd* in the Ugaritic fragments is ambiguous. Thus, at least in *KTU* 1.108, the word can also be translated as "demon," which corresponds to Akkadian *šēdu* and Hebrew and Aramaic שֵׁד / *šdy*[37] (borrowed from the Akkadian?). Second, there is no semantic connection between the biblical שׁדי אל and the Ugaritic "El of the Hunt." Of course, Yahweh also occasionally appears in the Hebrew Bible as "Lord of the Animals" (cf. Job 38–39);[38] but in this role he notably does *not* bear the name שׁדי.

(c) Temporally, geographically, and philologically closer to the Priestly Writing are the attestations for *šdyn*-creatures in the Aramaic inscription from Tell Deir ʿAlla in Transjordan, also known as the Balaam Inscription (*KAI* 312:6; *COS* 2.27:142).[39] As mentioned above, this inscription,

---

37. In the Hebrew Bible, the indeterminate word שֵׁד only occurs in Deut 32:17 and Ps 106:37 and has a negative connotation (on this and on the corresponding Aramaic attestations, see Reynolds, "What are Demons," 606–10). Vorländer, *Mein Gott*, 215–24, traced שׁדי itself back to שֵׁד (see already Nöldeke, "Anzeigen: Friedr. Delitzsch," 735–36; Cohen, *Religion*, 345–46), hypothesized an original vocalization of שֵׁדִי or שַׁדִּי, interpreted this as an indication of the deity's function, and thus proposed the translation "my protector god / my personal god." Even against the background of the rendering of שׁדי in the LXX of Genesis (see below), such an interpretation still seems debatable to me. The *šdyʾ* attested in inscriptions from Palmyra could also be associated with *šed* "demon" (see *DNWSI*, 1111, s.v. *šdy* 2).
38. On this, see esp. Keel, *Jahwes Entgegnung*.
39. Whether line 5 also contains the reading *šdyn* (*KAI* 5; Schüle, *Israels Sohn*, 129; Blum, "Kombination I," 577) is quite uncertain. Hoftijzer (in *TUAT* 2:141) and Jaroš, *Inschriften des Heiligen Landes*, no. 195, 299, conjecture *šgr*; Lutzky, "Shaddai," 26–31, reads *šdy* and understands this as "the one of the breast" and thus as an epithet of the goddess Asherah; see pp. 17–18.

which was written in ink on wall plaster, probably dates to the ninth/ eighth century BCE. The text, which is labeled as *spr blʿm* in the super-scription, could have also been transmitted on other written media such as papyrus and could have been known in later periods. Here, the *šdyn* are a group of gods in the divine council and possibly have a juridical function.[40] Here, too, the etymology is debated. The word should probably be associated with the aforementioned Hebrew and Aramaic word שַׁד / *šdy*.[41] The possibility that there is a traditio-historical and perhaps even literary-historical connection between the *šdyn* of the Deir ʿAlla Inscription and the biblical שׁדי, particularly in the references in the third and fourth Balaam oracles in Num 24:4, 16, cannot be ruled out. However, against a *direct* identification of the *šdyn* in the Deir ʿAlla Inscription with the biblical term שׁדי made on the basis of the parallel in Numbers 24,[42] it should be noted that the *šdyn* indicate a group that is subordinate to the deities El (line 2), Šagar (lines 5, 6[?], 14), and Aštar (line 14) and not an individual deity[43] (cf. the reference to the parallel group of the *ʾlhn* "gods" in line 5). Thus, the Transjordanian *šdyn* correspond more closely to the בני האלהים of the Hebrew Bible, who belong to Yahweh's royal household (Job 1:6–12, Ps 82).

(d) Finally, Donald B. Redford (1970) and Manfred Görg (1981/ 2001) have proposed a connection between the Egyptian word *šed* (*šd.w*) "savior" (derived from the verb *šdj* "to rescue"), which can also appear as a divine title,[44] and the Hebrew term שׁדי.[45] The proposed etymology cor-responds to the aspect of שׁדי as a "savior" (cf. Heb. מושיע in Isa 43:11, 45:15). Such an etymology is phonetically plausible and cannot be ruled out traditio-historically, since the Priestly Writing draws on Egyptian con-cepts in other places as well, as can be seen in the parallels between the Priestly account of creation by speech (Gen 1) and Egyptian cosmogonies.[46]

---

40. Thus the conjecture of Delcor, "Des inscriptions de Deir," 35.

41. Cf. *DNWSI*, 1111, and Reynolds, "What are Demons," 605–6.

42. In contrast, Delcor, "Des inscriptions de Deir," suggested that the author of Num 24 demythologized the *šdyn* insofar as he made שׁדי, like אל and עליון, into a title for Yahweh; similarly Levin, *Der Jahwist*, 386.

43. Thus apparently, however, Niehr, *Religionen in Israels Umwelt*, 210.

44. Erman and Grapow, *Wörterbuch*, IV, 563.

45. Redford, *A Study of the Biblical Story*, 129; Görg, "Šaddaj," 13–15; idem, Schaddai, 454–55; and Seebass, *Genesis II*, 100, who (with reference to the latter studies) also prefers to connect the *šdyn*-creatures in the Deir ʿAlla Inscription with the Egyptian word *šdj*. For an evalution of the thesis of Redford and Görg, see recently Neumann, "(El) Šadday," 248–51.

46. Cf., for example, the so-called "Monument of Memphite Theology" from the eighth century BCE, in which Ptah uses speech in the act of creation (*TUAT.E*: 166–75; *COS* 1.15:21–23).

(e) The biblical concept of a revelation of El in various forms, including as אל שׁדי, prior to the revelation of Yahweh, has misled prior research to reconstruct a pre-Yahwistic religion of Israel's ancestors on the basis of a traditio-historical analysis of the relevant texts in Genesis. The hypothesis of the worship of ancestral deities, which goes back especially to Albrecht Alt (1929),[47] has been fundamentally refuted by Matthias Köckert (1988),[48] such that it is not necessary to address this issue in detail here. A variant of this hypothesis was proposed by Klaus Koch (1976),[49] who argued that the divine name שׁדי was already at home among the Israelites who were gradually settling in southern Palestine in the early Iron Age and was connected with the ancestral deity at that point.[50] Such an idea has reappeared more recently in the works of Othmar Keel and Christoph Uehlinger (1992/2010) and Rainer Albertz (1996).[51]

It is equally unlikely that the Priestly Writing's literary and theological construction of Yahweh's initial self-revelation as אל שׁדי followed by the revelation of his true name in Exod 6:3 reflects a transition from a pre-Yahwistic veneration of the god El and his assistant שׁדי, as Harriet Lutzky (1998) proposed.[52] Thus far, there is no solid evidence for the worship of שׁדי before or alongside the worship of Yahweh, whether by proto-Israelites or in the cultures that surrounded ancient Israel. Rather, it can be assumed that the Priestly Writing was responsible for introducing אל שׁדי as a distinct figure not only at the literary level but also at the religio-historical level.

(f) To summarize the foregoing discussion: The etymology and origins of the divine title שׁדי remain obscure. The search for its linguistic derivation points to practically every language and religion in ancient Israel's cultural environs.[53] This search allows for correlations between the

---

47. Alt, *Gott der Väter.*
48. Köckert, *Vätergott und Väterverheißungen*; idem, "Gott der Väter," 915–19.
49. Klaus Koch, "ŠADDAJ," 118, 151; cf. Fohrer, *Das Buch Hiob*, 152–53.
50. Cf. Weippert, "שַׁדַּי Šaddaj," 881.
51. Keel and Uehlinger, *Göttinnen, Götter und Gottessymbole*, 237; Albertz, *Religionsgeschichte Israels*, vol. 1, 55–56. The thesis of Fritz Stolz, *Strukturen und Figuren*, 161, that El was שׁדי in the pre-Yahwistic Jerusalem cult just as the god Enlil was *šadû rabû* in Mesopotamia is likewise not supported by the textual evidence.
52. Lutzky, "Shadday," 34–35. On the theological-historical context of the Priestly conception in Exod 6:2–3, see de Pury, "Gott," 138–99, who understands the temporal and spatial diversity of the worship of God advocated by P as a response of Yahwistic religion to the Persian imperial theology.
53. Here I have left out the Arabian evidence, although it is possibly also of relevance if one interprets the Old North Arabian (Thamudic) personal name *ʾlśdy* as a reference to the biblical שׁדי (on this, see Knauf, "El Šaddaj," 22; and on the problem of dating this

biblical term שׁדי and different ancient Near Eastern gods and conceptions
of divinity but does not allow for a precise identification. These correlations exist on different linguistic, temporal, sociocultural, and theological
levels and thereby open a variety of windows into the world of ancient
Israel within the context of the ancient Near East and its deities. The
divine title שׁדי or אל שׁדי does not, however, allow for any conclusions
regarding a form of Israelite religion that existed prior to or alongside
Yahwism. Rather, it reflects different theological concepts that periodically
emerged under the influence of the Priestly Writing and its monotheism in
Jewish writings from the Persian and Hellenistic periods. Thus, the divine
title שׁדי only became part of the history of Israelite and Jewish religion
and theology in the sixth century BCE and the centuries that followed.

Precisely how the Priestly Writing itself conceived of the divine title
שׁדי is difficult to say. In light of its consistent use of שׁדי in the context
of the promise of fruitfulness and increase, it cannot be ruled out that
P in fact had in view the word שַׁד / שָׁדַיִם "breast" (cf. Gen 49:25, Ps
22:10–11), as Martin Luther had already suggested in his Genesis lecture
(1535/38), describing God as "a breast to cherish and nourish them [i.e.,
Israel]."[54] In any event, this thesis is not contradicted by the notion that
Yahweh is consistently conceived of as a male deity in the Hebrew Bible,
since sometimes female metaphors are applied to him (cf. Isa 66:13). On
the other hand, I find improbable the notion that *šdy* in the sense of "the
one of the breast" was originally an epithet of the goddess Asherah reflecting her aspect as a *dea nutrix* and was secondarily associated with El in the
name *El-Šdy* before finally becoming an epithet for Yahweh,[55] since such a
title for Asherah is not attested in Ugaritic and Canaanite sources.

In contrast to the Hebrew text, the Greek translations show much
more clearly how early Judaism understood the divine title שׁדי.

---

evidence [between the fifth century BCE and the fourth century CE!], see Niehr, "שַׁדַּי
šaddaj," 1082–83). As in the case of the Egyptian personal name *šadê-ʿammí* from the four-
teenth century BCE, which is occasionally invoked in interpreting the term שׁדי (cf. Cross,
Canaanite Myth, 53; see also p. 8 n. 5 above), I regard the evidence as too weak to support
far-reaching theories.

54. Luther, WA 42, 607, 29–32 ("ubera ad fovendos et alendos eos"). On this, see also
Ziemer, *Abram – Abraham*, 332, as well as Robert, "El Shaddaï," who, like Heinrich Ewald,
derives שׁדי from the root שׁדה (which is not attested in Biblical Hebrew, but cf. Aram. *šdʾ* "to
flow, overflow") and thus understands אל שׁדי as "Dieu fécondateur"—a meaning that is still
preserved in the older (sic!) books of Genesis and Job, while it has been lost in the later (sic!)
prophetic and psalmic texts, having been replaced by its identification with שׁדד.

55. Thus Lutzky, "Shadday," 15–36.

2. Pantokrator

2.1. *The Rendering of El Shaddai in the Ancient Greek Translations*

(a) In the Septuagint, the occurrences of אֵל שַׁדַּי in the Pentateuch are consistently rendered as θεός, generally with an additional possessive pronoun.[56] Thus, Gen 17:1 in the Septuagint does not read "I am אֵל שַׁדַּי" but rather "I am your God." The linguistic considerations that underlie this translation are unclear. Martin Rösel has proposed that, at least in the Septuagint of Genesis, θεός renders אֵל while the possessive pronoun renders the Aramaic relative particle *dî*, which can express a genitive relationship.[57] A problem with this thesis is that it does not explain the Hebrew שַׁ/שֶׁ. Thus, I would suggest that the rendering of אֵל שַׁדַּי as θεός σου / θεός μου / θεός αὐτῶν.[58] instead reflects an understanding of אֵל שַׁדַּי as a combination of the words אֵל and שֶׁד.[59] In this interpretation, the translators saw a close relationship between God and Israel's ancestors, which they highlighted through the use of the possessive pronoun. What Rösel's and my own linguistic explanations have in common is that they interpret the Septuagint translation as an attempt to transform the difficult expression אֵל שַׁדַּי into a relational statement in which God appears as the personal protector-god of the ancestors. Semantically, the Septuagint's understanding is appropriate to the context of the ancestral narratives. Thematically, however, the Septuagint's translation undermines the Priestly Writing's three-stage concept of revelation (יהוה—אֵל שַׁדַּי—אלהים) by harmonizing the ancestors' speeches about their God in Genesis.

(b) On one occasion in the Septuagint, שַׁדַּי is translated as ὁ ἱκανός (Ruth 1:20–21). In "Theodotion's" translation of the book of Job (first century CE[60]) and among certain church fathers, ὁ ἱκανός is consistently

---

56. Cf. Gen 17:1, 28:3, 35:11, 48:3, 49:25, Exod 6:3; on Num 24:4, 16; see nn. 58 and 59 below.

57. Martin Rösel, "Die Übersetzung der Gottesnamen," 373–74; on this, see also Bachmann, *Göttliche Allmacht*, 139.

58. The reading of the LXX in Exod 6:3 (θεὸς ὢν αὐτῶν; MT: בְּאֵל שַׁדַּי) probably has less to do with an aim of harmonizing the text with Exod 3:14 (ἐγώ εἰμι ὁ ὤν; MT: אֶהְיֶה אֲשֶׁר אֶהְיֶה) (thus Martin Rösel, "Theo-Logie," 56) than with an attempt to translate the *beth essentiae* in בְּאֵל שַׁדַּי (cf. Isa 26:4, Ps 68:5; and on this Hartenstein, "Die Geschichte JHWHs," 88–89) appropriately.

59. Cf. the corresponding rendering of the short form שַׁדַּי with θεός alone and without a possessive pronoun in Num 24:4, 16 and Isa 13:6; similarly also (cautiously) Klaus Koch, "ŠADDAJ," 127.

60. On this, see Gentry, *The Asterisked Materials*, 494–99; on the dependence of LXX Ruth on the *kaige*-Theodotion tradition, see Tov, "Three Dimensions of LXX," 540.

used as the equivalent for שׁדּי.[61] The translation of שׁדּי by ὁ ἱκανός is based linguistically in the splitting of שׁדּי into the relative particle שׁ and the predicate דּי, such that שׁדּי signifies "(the one) who is sufficient." Correspondingly, a literal translation of ὁ ἱκανός in the LXX would mean "the self-sufficient one."[62] Conceptually, this corresponds to the Hellenistic notion of the self-sufficiency of the deity, which found classic expression in the words of Euripides (ca. 480–406 BCE):

> For the deity, if he be really such, has no wants.[63]

The Jewish philosopher Philo of Alexandria (25 BCE–ca. 50 CE) explicitly takes up this conception in his theology.[64] Structural parallels to such etymologizing are found in the aforementioned verse Isa 13:6 (par. Joel 1:15), which connects שׁדּי with the word שׁדּ or in the explanation of the tetragrammaton through the verb היה ("to be") in Exod 3:14. A similar example from Classical Greek literature is the explanation of the name Zeus through the preposition διά and the verb ζῆν, which is already presupposed by Plato in the dialogue *Cratylus* (396a–b) and which found its classical expression among the Stoics:

> They give the name Dia (Δία) because all things are due to (δία) him; Zeus (Ζῆνα) in so far as he is the cause of life (ζῆν) or pervades all life. (Diogenes Laertius, *Lives* 7.147 = *SVF* 2.1021)[65]

The explanation of שׁדּי as a combination of שׁ and דּי left a deep impression in postbiblical Judaism that can be traced from *Genesis Rabbah*[66] (a

---

61. Cf. Epiphanius, *Pan.* 2.86.12 (Σαδδαι ὁ ἱκανός), Theodoret, *Haer. fab.* 83.460.13 (Σαδδαι = ὁ ἱκανός καὶ δύνατος); on this, see also the Greek variants of Ezek 1:24, 10:5 cited on p. 12 nn. 18 and 19 above.

62. Cf. Tov, "Three Dimensions of LXX," 540: "He who is sufficient-competent"; LSJ and LEH offer the freer translations of "the Almighty" and "the Mighty One," respectively.

63. Euripides, *Herc.* 1345–46, trans. E. P. Coleridge (in Oates and O'Neill, *The Complete Greek Drama*, vol. 1); cf. Plato, *Lysis*, 215a.

64. Philo, *Cher.* 46, *Leg.* 1.44, *Mut.* 46; on this, see Bertram, "ΙΚΑΝΟΣ," 20–31.

65. Diogenes Laertius, *Lives*, trans. R. D. Hicks (Lives. vol. 2, 250–51); see also as a quote of Chrysipp, *SVF* 2.1062, 1076.

66. "'Abraham,' said God to him, 'let it suffice thee that I am thy God; let it suffice thee that I am thy Patron, and not only for thee alone, but it is sufficient for My world that I am its God and its Patron.' / R. Nathan said in R. Aha's name, and R. Berekiah said in R. Isaac's name: I AM EL SHADDAI (GOD ALMIGHTY): It is I who said to My world, '*day*' (enough)! And had I not said '*day*!' to My world, the heaven would still have been spreading and the earth would have gone on expanding to this very day. / It was taught in the name of R. Eliezer b. Jacob: It is I whose Godhead outweighs the world and the fulness thereof. Akilas translated it: Sufficient and incomparable." (Gen. Rab. XLVI.3, trans. H. Freedman, *Midrash Rabbah*, 389–90).

Midrash) through the medieval commentators[67] up to Samson Raphael Hirsch (1867): here, שדי shifts from "the 'Sufficient One'" to the God who reveals the boundaries of all creation.[68]

(c) In both of its occurrences in the Psalms, the Greek translators placed שדי in a direct relationship with the celestial power of God and translated the term according to its context. Thus, the translator of Ps 68:15 employs the word ὁ ἐπουράνιος ("the Heavenly One"), which was used already by Homer as a designation for the gods[69] but which appears only rarely in the Septuagint and, with the exception of Ps 68[67], is only attested in genuinely Greek texts.[70] The translator of Ps 91[90] renders שדי as ὁ θεὸς τοῦ οὐρανοῦ ("the God of heaven").[71]

Yahweh's connection to "heaven" corresponds to the ancient Near Eastern conception of *bʿl šmm*, the lord of heaven, which was widespread in the region of Syria–Canaan (and beyond) during the first millennium BCE.[72] In the context of the Septuagint, it finds its counterpart in the description of Zeus as ἐπουράνιος,[73] who, as a weather god in ancient Greek religion, had power over hail, snow, and torrential rains, just as in Ps 68.[74]

Most striking is the rendering of שדי with the terms ὁ κύριος "the Lord" and ὁ παντοκράτωρ "the Almighty" in the Septuagint version of

---

67. See, for example, Rashi's explanation of Gen 17:1: "*I am the almighty God*, I am the one who in my power looks after all creation (*Gen. Rab.*); . . . and everywhere this verse appears, this is its interpretation: He is sufficient; always in accordance with the context" (Commentary on the Pentateuch, 45).

68. Samson Rapahel Hirsch, *Der Pentateuch*, vol. 1, 240–41; cf. Cohen, *Religion*, 45.

69. Homer, *Od.* 17.484, *Il.* 6.129, 6.131, 6.527. For further examples from Greek literature, cf. Theocritus, *Id.* 25.5; Moschus Syracusanus, *Europe* 21; SEG 31, 1080 (Ancyra, third century CE?).

70. 2 Macc 3:39, 3 Macc 6:28, 7:6, 4 Macc 4:11, 11:3; for further references in Jewish and Christian literature see *3 Bar.* 11:9, Pr Man 1 (Cod. A), *T. Abr.* A 2:3, 17:11, *T. Job* 40:3, *Sib. Or.* 1:216, 2:222, 2:284, 4:51, 4:135, 8:66; frag. 1:10; *Odes* 14:11, *Ps.-Orph.* 39 (in Denis, *Fragmenta*, 166, line 18), *FragmAnonym* 574.3042 (in Denis, *Fragmenta*, 237, line 24), Matt 18:35 (v.l.) and on this Lightfoot, *The Sibylline Oracles*, 537.

71. In the OT, see Gen 24:3, 7; 2 Chr 36:23; Ezra 1:2, 5:11–12, 6:9–10; Neh 1:4–5, 2:4, 20; Ps 136:26; Dan 2:18–19, 37, 44, 4:34; Jonah 1:9; Tob 5:17, 10:11; Jdt 5:8, 6:19, 11:17; as well as in the Elephantine Papyri APFC 30:2, 27, 31:2, 27, 32:3, 38:2, 3, 5, 40:1.

72. Cf. *KAI* 4:3; 18:1, 7; 26:III.18; 64:1; 202:11; 266:2; SAA 2 5:IV.10′ and on this Niehr, *Der höchste Gott*, 49–60.

73. For the inscriptional evidence, cf. SGUÄ 4166; Inscriptions from Nikaia (Sencer, *Iznik Müzesi*), no. 1114 (fourth century CE); no. 1115 (third century CE). The description of Zeus as οὐράνιος is more frequently attested; cf. Pindar, *Paean.* 52u9; Callimachus, *Hymn. Jov.* 55; *Epigr.* 52.3, AG 9.352.4, 16.293.3, AG Append. 199.15, 267.21; on this motif, see also Plato, *Phaedr.* 246e and on the latter, Cook, *Zeus*, II/2, 1338.

74. Cf. Homer, *Il.* 12.278–280; Pindar, *Isthm.* 4.17; Aeschylus, *Sept.* 212; on this, see also Brown, *Israel and Hellas*, II, 68–69.

Job;[75] here I will only discuss the divine title παντοκράτωρ in detail.

2.2. The Religio-Historical Context of the Divine Title Pantokrator

(a) The majority of the attestations of παντοκράτωρ in the Old Testament go back to the Hebrew word צבאות,[76] which (with a few exceptions) is only translated as παντοκράτωρ in the Book of the Twelve and the book of Jeremiah[77] but not in the Psalms or in the book of Isaiah. As in the case of the rendering of שׁדי with παντοκράτωρ, which is restricted to the Septuagint version of Job, it can be concluded that the Septuagint was produced by different circles of translators from different time periods and geographical areas, each of which had its own particular theological perspective.[78] Beyond its use in the Greek translation of the Hebrew Bible, the term παντοκράτωρ is concentrated in certain Hellenistic Jewish writings (Judith, 2 Maccabees, 3 Maccabees; strikingly rare in Sirach, Wisdom, and Philo, completely absent in Josephus).[79] It often occurs in lists of divine names and epithets. In every case, the term παντοκράτωρ, corresponding to its etymology, represents the all-encompassing authority of God that is expressed in his actions as creator, judge, and protective warrior deity.

(b) The word παντοκράτωρ is not securely attested in Greek literature prior to its use in the Septuagint.[80] Thus, it cannot be ruled out that it is an innovation of the Septuagint through which the Hebraic/Jewish tradition

---

75. (ὁ) κύριος as an equivalent for שׁדי: Job 6:4, 14, 21:20, 22:3, 23, 26; 24:1, 31:3; (ὁ) παντοκράτωρ as an equivalent for שׁדי: Job 5:17, 8:5, 11:7, 15:25, 22:17, 25, 23:16, 27:2, 11, 13; 32:8, 33:4, 34:10, 12, 35:13, 37:22. In one case (Job 8:3), שׁדי is rendered by ὁ τὰ ποιήσας. In Job 5:8, ὁ κύριος ὁ πάντων δεσπότης (Cod. A παντοκράτωρ) probably reflects the reading אל אלהים.

76. On the interpretation of this term as the plural of צבא ("army") and on the religio-historical background, see *HAL* 3:934–35; Mettinger, "Yahweh Zebaoth," 920–24; Hartenstein, "Die Geschichte JHWHs," 83–84.

77. It is possible that Jeremiah and the Book of the Twelve were produced by the same translator (Tov, "Three Dimensions of LXX," 535).

78. On this, see also Martin Rösel, "Theo-Logie," 49–62.

79. Jdt 4:13, 8:13, 15:10, 16:5, 17; 2 Macc 1:25, 3:22, 30, 5:20, 6:26, 7:35, 38, 8:11, 18, 24; 15:8, 32; 3 Macc 2:2, 8, 5:7, 6:2, 18, 28; Jer 39:19 LXX, Bar 3:1, 4, Esth 4:17b LXX, Wis 7:25, Sir 42:17 (κύριος ὁ παντοκράτωρ; H[B] אלהים צבאיו; H[Mas] אדני), 50:14 (ὕψιστος παντοκράτωρ; H[B] עליון), 50:17 (παντοκράτωρ θεὸς ὕψιστος; H[B] עליון . . . קדוש ישראל), Pr Man 1, *Ep. Arist.* 185:2, *3 Bar.* 1:3, *Par. Jer.* 1:5, 9:6, *T. Abr.* A 8:3, 15:12, *Sib. Or.* 1:66, 2:220, 2:330, 8:82, 8:265, 11:8, in Philo only in *Sacr.* 63.2, *Gig.* 64.7 and in *Som.* 2.172 as a quotation of Isa 5:7; in contrast, the term πανηγεμών appears frequently in Philo: Congr 117.1, *Migr.* 175.3, *Sobr.* 57.2–3, *Plant.* 58.1, *Agr.* 50.3, *Post.* 5.2, 9.6; on this see also Bousset and Gressmann, *Religion*, 312; Bachmann, *Göttliche Allmacht*, 174–82; Zimmermann, *Die Namen des Vaters*, 247–56, and on the use of παντοκράτωρ in the Greek book of Sirach, see Mulder, "Two Approaches," 221–34 (esp. pp. 223–24).

80. The reading παντοκρα[. . .] in the Aeschylus-Fragment 168* with reference to Zeus is uncertain; for the text, see Radt, *Tragicorum Graecorum Fragmenta*; OxyPap

was adapted to the Greek/pagan context and subsequently worked its way into its broader pagan environment. A linguistic precursor to παντοκράτωρ is the word παγκρατής, which appears in pagan choral songs, cultic hymns, and dedicatory inscriptions. Thus, παγκρατής appears as an epithet for Zeus in the works of Aeschylus (525–456 BCE), Sophocles (497–405 BCE), and Euripides (480–406 BCE), in the Hymn of Mt. Dikte (third century BCE?), in the hymn to Zeus by the Stoic Cleanthes (331–232 BCE), or in the hymn to Hera by the poet Bacchylides (ca. 505–450 BCE).[81] In addition are variants such as ὁ πάντων κύριος / ὁ ἁπάντων κύριος with reference to Zeus in the works of Pindar (ca. 522–446 BCE)[82] or ὁ πάντων κρατῶν, also with reference to Zeus, in the writings of Aelius Aristides (117–189 CE).[83] The use of the term παντοκράτειρα with reference to the goddess Isis in Isidor's first hymn to Isis comes directly from the context of the Septuagint.[84] The same is true of the term παγκράτωρ with reference to the Egyptian crocodile god Suchos (Egyptian Sobek/sehu; cf. fig. 2) in Isidor's fourth hymn to Isis (ca. 80 BCE)[85] as well as to the goddess Gē/

[XVIII] no. 2164 frag. 1:14 [second century CE]; see also Bachmann, *Göttliche Allmacht*, 153; Lightfoot, *The Sibylline Oracles*, 542; Zimmermann, *Die Namen des Vaters*, 234, 236).

81. Cf. Aeschylus, *Sept.* 255; *Suppl.* 816; *Eum.* 918; Sophocles, *Phil.* 679; *fr.* 684.4; Euripides, *Fr.* 431.4; hymn to Zeus of Mt. Dikta (Furley and Bremer, *Greek Hymns*, I, 68–75; II, 1–20); Cleanthes, *fr.* 1.1; or Bacchylides, *Epinicia* 11.44; on the hymnic address of a deity as παγκρατής in pagan literature, see also Roscher, *Ausführliches Lexikon*, III/1, 1535; Montevecchi, "Pantokrator," 402; Hommel, "Pantokrator," 140–51 (with the thesis that the Stoics no longer understood παγκρατής in the sense of "all powerful" but rather as "all sustaining," which is also occasionally attested in the later Jewish and Christian usage of παντοκράτωρ, such as in *Ep. Arist.* 185.2 but especially in the Apostles' Creed); Furley and Bremer, *Greek Hymns*, II, 6, and Zimmermann, *Die Namen des Vaters*, 234–36.

82. Pindar, *Isthm.* 5.53; cf. Demosthenes, *Epitaph.* 21.6 and Plutarch, *Mor.* 426a as well as Diodorus Siculus 3.61.4 (Zeus as κύριος τῶν ὅλων); applied to Osiris by Plutarch, *Mor.* 355e; for further attestations see Zeller, "Κυριος κύριος," 493; for further transliterations, see Montevecchi, "Pantokrator," 402.

83. Aelius Aristides, *Hymn to Zeus* 8.28; see also the scholion on παγκρατής in Aeschylus, *Sept.* 255 (O. L. Smith, *Scholia Graeca*, vol. 2.2), as well as an inscription from Delos (*SIG³* III:1138: Διὶ τῷ πάντων κρατοῦντι καὶ Μητρὶ μεγάλῃ τῇ πάντων κρατούσῃ).

84. SEG 8.548.2 (= SGUÄ 8138.2 = Totti, *Ausgewählte Texte*, no. 21, line 2); P.Oxy. 1380.20 (= Totti, *Ausgewählte Texte*, no. 20, line 20); on this, see also Zimmermann, *Die Namen des Vaters*, 237.

85. SEG 8.551.23 (= Totti, *Ausgewählte Texte*, no. 24, line 23). On the cult of Suchos in the Hellenistic and Roman periods, see also Roeder, *Kulte und Orakel*, 299–303, or the description in Strabo, *The Geography*, 17.1.38: "Sailing along to the distance of 100 stadia, we come to the city Arsinoë, formerly called Crocodilopolis; for the inhabitants of this nome worship the crocodile. The animal is accounted sacred, and kept apart by himself in a lake; it is tame, and gentle to the priests, and is called Suchus. It is fed with bread, flesh, and wine, which strangers who come to see it always present" (trans. H. C. Hamilton and W. Falconer). Among the numerous attestations for the worship of Suchos listed in SGUÄ, special reference should be made to nos. 13871 (priest of Suchos; ca. 200–150 BCE); 8885 and 8887 (both Ptolemaios X Alexander I); as well as 15086 (Tiberius) and 1007 (Vespasian); on this,

Gaia in a burial epigram from Alexandria (first century BCE).[86]

All further occurrences of παντοκράτωρ / παντοκράτειρα in non-Jewish literature, whether with reference to Zeus, Hermes, Isis, Physis, Pluto, Persephone, the Egyptian sun-god Mandulis (Egyp. *mrwr/mrwl*), or Sarapis,[87] are found in texts from the Common Era.[88] Whether the invocation κύριος παντοκράτωρ on an epitaph from Neoclaudiopolis (Paphlagonia, ca. 230 CE) refers to Helios or to the Christian deity is uncertain.[89]

(c) On account of its use in the book of Judith as well as in 2 and 3 Maccabees,[90] Reinhard Feldmeier has proposed that the term παντοκράτωρ reflects a reaction of Hellenistic Judaism against the universal claim to rule first by Alexander the Great (356–323 BCE), then by the nascent kingdoms of the Diadochoi, and finally by the Roman Empire.[91] The term παντοκράτωρ would thus have been an expression of the political theology of Hellenistic Judaism. I do not rule out this religio-political derivation of the title Pantokrator, particularly considering that the term παντοκράτωρ sometimes renders the divine title צבאות, which has military connotations. However, several other elements must also be taken into consideration, including the ancient Near Eastern heritage of the Septuagint translators, the aforementioned linguistic precursors in Classical Greek literature, and the religious aims of the Septuagint translators.

see also the papyri that were found in the temple of Suchos in Tebtunis, the "City (κώμη) of Suchos" (P.Tebtunis 281).

86. SGUÄ 8960.12.

87. Zeus: Inscriptions from Nikaia (Sencer, *Iznik Müzesi*), no. 1121 (third century CE); no. 1512 (second to third centuries CE); an inscription from Ephesus (Engelmann, *Die Inschriften von Ephesos*), no. 1262 (an undated inscription referring to Zeus Polieus).

Hermes: Epigr. Gr. 815.11 (= AG App. Epigr. dedicatoria 237.11: Eriounios); PGM 7.668.

Isis: *IG* V.2.472 (Megalopolis, second to third centuries CE).

Physis: *Hymn. Orph.* 10.4.

Pluto: *Hymn. Orph.* 18.17.

Persephone: *Hymn. Orph.* 29.10.

Mandulis: Hymn from the temple of Mandulis in Talmis (Kalabsha) (SGUÄ 4127).

Sarapis: P.Berlin Inv.-No. 21227 (origin unknown, third/fourth century; Horsley, *New Documents* 3, 118).

88. In the NT, παντοκράτωρ only occurs in 2 Cor 6:18 in a quotation of 2 Sam 7:8 and 2 Sam 7:14 (MT: יהוה צבאות, G: κύριος παντοκράτωρ) and nine times in the book of Revelation, which uses the term—as was common in Hellenistic Judaism—in the context of praising God as creator and judge (Rev 1:8, 4:8 [cf. Isa 6:3], 11:17, 15:3, 16:7, 14, 19:6 [cf. Ezek 1:24], 19:15, 21:22); for detailed treatments of this, see Montevecchi, "Pantokrator," 418–20; Aune, *Revelation 1–5*, 57–58; Bachmann, *Göttliche Allmacht*, 182–95; Zimmermann, *Die Namen des Vaters*, 257–69.

89. SEG 50.1233.

90. See n. 79 above (p. 22).

91. Feldmeier, "Almighty," 20–21; idem, "Nicht Übermacht noch Impotenz," 24–28.

Fig. 2. Stela commemorating the establishment of a youth center under Ptolemy [X] Alexander [I], who is depicted as offering before Sobek, ca. 106–88 BCE. From Roeder, *Die ägyptische Götterwelt*, 203.

Thus, in the Jewish usage of the title παντοκράτωρ, three components are combined: (1) ancient Near Eastern conceptions of divine authority as attested from the third millennium BCE up to the Roman period, (2) the reception and modification of Greek terminology, and (3) a confrontation with the Hellenistic phenomenon—especially prominent in Egypt—of ascribing all-encompassing competencies to individual supreme deities. At a later period, as Christiane Zimmermann has shown, the use of the title παντοκράτωρ in Judaism and Christianity could have also served as a critical reflex against the term αὐτοκράτωρ, which was important in the Roman cult of the emperor.[92] Thus, in Hellenistic Judaism, the title of Pantokrator combines the elements of "tradition" (with respect to the ancient Near Eastern heritage), "innovation" (with respect to linguistic form), and "apologetics" (with respect to the claims of the Hellenistic rulers *and* of the Hellenistic supreme deities).

---

92. Zimmermann, *Die Namen des Vaters*, 238–40.

3. Conclusion

Like the Hebrew Bible and the Old Testament as a whole, the divine title אל שדי (which was presumably introduced by the Priestly Writing in the sixth/fifth century BCE) and the title παντοκράτωρ coined by the Septuagint have a double history of reception.

In rabbinic Judaism, the divine name שדי is used relatively rarely, although it is more prominent in Jewish magical and mystical texts. Thus, as already in Ps 91 and 4Q511, שדי is found together with other divine names in late antique amulets and incantation bowls.[93] Corresponding to the use of the name in the book of Genesis, here שדי is invoked in the context of fruitfulness and divine protection. The term also occurs occasionally in medieval Jewish wisdom literature, such as in the Wisdom text from the Cairo Geniza 1:12, 8:15, 11:18, 16:18.[94]

The multidimensional translation work of Jewish theologians in the second/first century BCE served as the foundation for the use of the divine title παντοκράτωρ in Greek-speaking Judaism of late antiquity,[95] its use with respect to different deities in the Greek magical papyri from Egypt,[96] and especially the use of the title "Pantokrator" in the Christian confession of faith and the designation of Jesus Christ as παντοκράτωρ,[97] which later found iconographic expression in the Byzantine depictions of Christ the Pantokrator (cf. fig. 3).

The fact that Martin Luther consistently translated every occurrence of אל שדי / שדי in the Old Testament as "the Almighty" ultimately stands

---

93. Naveh and Shaked, *Magic Spells*, amulet no. 28; bowl no. 19; idem, *Amulets and Magic Bowls*, amulet No. 4; amulet No. 12; Nestler, *Die Kabbala*, 74–110 (esp. 90–91).

94. On the dating and the contextualization of this text within the history of philosophy, see Rüger, *Die Weisheitsschrift*, 15–19.

95. On this, see the texts cited in n. 79 (p. 22) as well as the synagogue inscriptions from Sardis and Gorgippia (in Trebilco, *Jewish Communities*, 45–46; SEG 51:1635–57; esp. no. 1646). On the debate over the Jewish or pagan background of this inscription see Montevecchi, "Pantokrator," 403–4; Bachmann, *Göttliche Allmacht*, 155.

96. For example: PGM 3.218, 4.272, 7.668, 7.962, 12.238, 12.250, 13.761, 22a.19, 71.3 (*Iao*), 8a rec.1 (*Iao Sabaoth*), among others. For a detailed discussion, see Montevecchi, "Pantokrator," 413–418 and the following note.

97. For the description of Jesus as Pantokrator see, for example, Clement of Alexandria, *Paed.* 1,9,84,1; Origen, *Fr. Ps.*, Ps 23:10, or Athanasius, *Orationes tres contra Arianos* (PG 26.329.16–18), but also PGM 13a1, 21.43 (for further attestations in patristic literature, see Montevecchi, "Pantokrator," 424–430 and Bachmann, *Göttliche Allmacht*, 199–200). On the three dimensions that must be taken into account in the lexicography of the LXX, but also with regard to the intertextuality of the LXX—(1) the intention of the original Greek translator that led to the choice of the corresponding word in the translation, (2) the reception of this rendering within the LXX, which occasionally resulted in completely new intertextual relations not found in the Hebrew *Vorlage*, and (3) the use of this word in the NT and in patristic literature—see Tov, "Three Dimensions of LXX," 529–44.

Fig. 3. Master of Daphni, ca. 1100, mosaic in the Daphni monastery. From: The Yorck Project, *Die Bibel in der Kunst*, p. 2828.

in the wake of Alexandrian theology. Here, the aspects of divine provision and the relativizing of power that are derived from the history of the Israelite-Jewish divine titles שׁדי and παντοκράτωρ should also not be left out of consideration in the modern critiques of the profession of faith to God the Almighty. As the framing of the epithet παντοκράτωρ with the attributes "just" and "eternal" in the model doxology in 2 Macc 1:24–25 shows, the profession of God's justice and constancy are essential aspects of the discourse about the almighty God:

> [24] O Lord, Lord God, Creator of all things, you are awe-inspiring and strong and just and merciful, you alone are king and are kind. [25] You alone are bountiful, you alone are just and almighty and eternal (δίκαιος καὶ παντοκράτωρ καὶ αἰώνιος). You rescue Israel from every evil; you chose the ancestors and consecrated them.

CHAPTER 2

From Divine Justice to Human Justice

> Even apart from what can be observed historically, the idea of justice only arose in order to ponder the relationships in human community life, and the characteristic feature of justice is everywhere originally applied to a deity that stood in relation to human social ties. — Wolf Wilhelm Graf Baudissin[1]

1. Introduction

Justice is one of the central theological themes of the Old Testament. It occurs in every area of tradition and in a broad range of literary layers of the Old Testament, albeit with different points of emphasis. It is thus with good reason that Walter Dietrich has spoken of justice as the common thread that runs through the Old Testament.[2] Justice is a prominent theme already in the oldest cultic poetry from the monarchic period, which in turn reflects even older ancient Near Eastern concepts that reach back to the Late Bronze Age. For example, in Ps 89:15, צדק ומשפט, "justice and law," are described as the foundation of Yahweh's throne, which bears direct connections with Mesopotamian, Egyptian, and Hittite concepts from the second millennium BCE. Likewise, justice is a major topic in the very late theodicy passages in Ben Sira and in the Wisdom of Solomon, both of which reflect the encounter between Judaism and Hellenistic thought during the second/first century BCE.[3] Justice is a key concept

---

1. "Auch abgesehen von dem, was sich geschichtlich beobachten läßt, ist die Idee der Gerechtigkeit nur entstanden zu denken in den Beziehungen eines Gemeinschaftslebens der Menschen, und die Eigenschaft der Gerechtigkeit wird ursprünglich überall einer solchen Gottheit zugesprochen worden sein, die zu einem menschlichen Verbande in einem Verhältnis stand" (Baudissin, "Der gerechte Gott," 1–23, here: 16).
2. Dietrich, "Der rote Faden," 13–28.
3. Cf., respectively, Sir 5:4–8, 15:11–20, 33:7–15, 40:19 (on this, see Beentjes, "Theodicy," 509–24) and Wis 1:1–5:23, 12:1–27 (on this, see Winston, "Theodicy in the Wisdom of Solomon," 525–45).

28

in the story of Abraham (cf. Gen 15:6, 18:20–33), in the prophetic books, in Wisdom literature, and of course in the legal corpora of the Old Testament (cf. esp. the so-called Covenant Code in Exod 20–23*, the laws of Deuteronomy, and the Holiness Code in Lev 17–26). From the canonical perspective of the Hebrew Bible, the theme of justice ties together the canonical units of *Torah* and *Nevi'im*, which can be seen especially clearly in the *inclusio* created by Gen 6:9, Deut 32:4, and Mal 3:20.

> These are the descendants of Noah. Noah was *a righteous man* (צדיק), *blameless* (תמים) in his generation; Noah walked with God. (Gen 6:9)
> The Rock (i.e., God), his work is *perfect* (תמים), and all his ways are *just* (משפט). A faithful God, without deceit, *just and upright* (צדיק וישר) is he. (Deut 32:4)
> But for you who revere my name (i.e., God's name) *the sun of righteousness* (שמש צדקה) shall rise, with healing in its wings. You shall go out leaping like calves from the stall. (Mal 3:20 [4:2])

Outside the Pentateuch, the order of the individual books in the Greek and Latin biblical manuscripts and printed editions is highly variable, such that the compositional arc spanning from Gen 6:9 to Mal 3:20 is only evident in certain manuscripts of the Septuagint and Vulgate. Insofar as the book of Malachi concludes the Old Testament canon, as in many modern translations of the Bible, which ultimately reflect the order of books in the Paris Bible (thirteenth century), the theme of justice frames the Old Testament as a whole.[4]

Of fundamental importance is the fact that the Hebrew terms for justice (צדק, צדקה, and occasionally משור) and law (משפט), like the Akkadian word pair *kittu* and *mišaru* in Mesopotamia and the word *ma'at* in Egypt, are relational concepts.[5] To that effect, following Diethelm Michel, the terms can be further differentiated: צדק indicates "justice" as an abstract concept, while צדקה stands for an individual act of justice, and the plural can take on the meaning of "just deeds," whether with reference to God (cf. Ps 103:6, Dan 9:16) or humanity (cf. Ps 11:7, Dan 9:18).[6]

---

4. On the problem of the order of the individual books within the canon, see Brandt, *Endgestalten*.

5. See the review of research in Schmid, *Gerechtigkeit als Weltordnung*, 66–69, 182–86.

6. Michel, *Grundlegung einer hebräischen Syntax, Teil 1*, 65–66; for a detailed discussion, see idem, *Begriffsuntersuchung*; Crüsemann, "Gerechtigkeit," 427–50; Koch, "Ṣādaq," 37–64, here: p. 61. For additional terms in the lexical field of "justice" and for derivatives of שפט ("to judge") und ישר ("to be upright"), see Scharbert, "Gerechtigkeit I," 404–11; Niehr, *Herrschen und Richten*.

In the Old Testament, justice always describes a relationship between two entities. When applied to God, the terms for justice can be used with reference to the relationship between God and the world, between God and society, or between God and individuals. Correspondingly, when applied to humanity, justice can refer to the relationship between an individual and the world, between an individual and God, or between an individual and society. The relational aspect of justice gives it a dynamic and process-driven character. That is to say, justice can increase and decrease, it can be attributed or denied, and therefore ultimately remains elusive.

The motif of justice in the Old Testament has two axes: divine justice and human justice. Both axes involve—albeit with different emphases—cosmological, historical, anthropological, theological, and ethical dimensions. Both axes share three further aspects: the belief in justice, the problematizing of justice, and the redefining of justice. The progression of these three aspects is found both in the final form of the Old Testament as well as in different compositional layers of particular blocks of tradition, individual books, or entire groups of books and in this respect constitutes an inner-biblical dialogue on justice. In what follows, this will be shown through five case studies from five different areas of tradition in the Old Testament (Pentateuch, Historical books, Prophets, Wisdom books, and Apocrypha) with a view to a biblical theology—that is, a theology inherent to the biblical texts (the historical aspect)—and a theology that corresponds to the biblical texts (the systematic aspect). In doing so, I will also refer to the older texts and traditions that underlie the final form of the text through a historical process of reading—a process that is suggested by the biblical texts themselves and that can already be assumed for the texts' ancient authors and readers.[7]

2. The Case of Cain

I see that the world was not created by mercy, and it is not guided by the fruits of good works, and there is partiality in judgment. [. . .] There is no judgment and no judge, and there is no other world, and no giving of good reward to the righteous, and there is no punishment of the wicked.[8]

---

7. See, for example, the dates in the superscriptions to the prophetic books (cf. Isa 1:1, 6:1, Jer 1:1–3, Ezek 1:1–3 et al.), the linking of individual psalms to events in David's life (cf. Ps 18:1, 34:1, 51:1, 54:1–2 et al.), or direct quotations from the book of Jeremiah in later books (cf. Dan 9:2, 2 Chr 35:25, 36:12).

8. *Targum Neofiti*, trans. Eldon Clem (Accordance 11.2.5., OakTree Software 2016/2017).

The author of *Targum Neofiti 1*—an early medieval Aramaic translation of the Torah that probably originated in Palestine and that is full
of embellishments going far beyond the biblical text itself—placed these
words in the mouth of Cain when he converses with his brother Abel in
the field (Gen 4:8). This dispute between Cain (whose name means "the
creature," based on its derivation from the root קנה in Gen 4:1[9]) and his
brother Abel (הבל, "the fleeting one") over the justice of the creator deity
is probably a free invention of the Targum. Nevertheless, the Targumist
has found the nerve of the primeval paradigm in Gen 4: justice and creation are intimately connected to each other. Cain, "the creature" who,
according to the biblical narrator, was born of the primeval mother Eve
and God himself (Gen 4:1)—Cain, the archetype and reflection of humanity in its relation to God, the world, and fellow humans—expects,
as the creator's creature, to be treated in a way befitting this relationship;
he *expects justice*. For Cain, creation requires justice, or in other words,
creation is the expression of divine justice. In this respect, the biblical
figure of Cain, like his Targumic successor, is firmly rooted in an important biblical and ancient Near Eastern worldview: creation is the first act
of divine justice insofar as creation reveals the will of God or the gods to
the community. In the Old Testament, as in the ancient Near East, com-
munication is part of a deity's very nature.[10] While it is possible for a deity
in the ancient Near East to become solitary or impassive, in so doing the
deity loses part of his or her divinity.

Against this background, the opening of the Old Testament with two
creation narratives in Gen 1–4 (sic)[11] stemming from different groups of
tradents—one from a priestly milieu and one from a sapiential context,
without this being stated explicitly—is a powerful profession of divine justice and of the relationship established between God, the world, and humanity. Yet, questions begin to arise regarding this belief in divine justice,
first in muted form and then more explicitly. Thus, the human experience
of inequality that is explored in the figure of Cain is already detectible in
the background of the sevenfold priestly declaration that creation is good,
indeed very good (Gen 1:31), as well as in the sapiential test of the prime-

---

9. See Witte, *Die biblische Urgeschichte*, 166–71.
10. A certain exception here is the Egyptian god Aten in the context of the mono-
theistically oriented solar theology of Akhenaten, yet this remains an isolated episode in the
religious history of the ancient Near East; see Sternberg-el Hotabi, " 'Die Erde entsteht,' "
45–78, here: 53–59.
11. Generally, the creation narratives in Genesis are identified as Gen 1:1–2:4a and
Gen 2:4b–3:24, although the thematic thread of these narratives continues up to the birth
of Enosh ("human"/"mortal") in 4:25–26; see Gertz, "Von Adam zu Enosch," 215–36.

val human, Adam, over whether he can be led astray from trusting in God by the prospect of universal knowledge (Gen 3). Inequality, expressed in the perception of inadequate treatment of the creature that brings gifts to its creator (Gen 4:3–5), appears as a rupture in the relationship between creator and creature and leads tragically to a rupture in the social relationships among fellow humans. In the words of Nelly Sachs, Cain becomes a "brother without a brother."[12] In contrast, the relationship to God remains intact since God preserves it, a notion that the sapiential narrator expresses through the mythic motif of God questioning the self-absorbed Cain (Gen 4:9–15). God is and remains the guarantor of justice, even if (and precisely because) humanity lacks a reason for living, which is described as a "sin" (חטאת) in Gen 4:7. The story of Cain and Abel emerges here as a condensed prolepsis of the multifaceted discourse on justice in the Joseph story (Gen 37–50).

In the legal texts and social laws of the Old Testament (cf. Exod 22:21–26, Deut 1:17),[13] but also in certain sapiential sayings (cf. Prov 22:22–23) and liturgical confessions (cf. Ps 7:12), the concept of the divine guarantee of justice, particularly toward the poor, emerges whenever the source of justice is traced directly back to Yahweh as the ultimate judge (שפט, Gen 18:25). From the perspective of the history of Israelite religion, this process can be described as a "theologizing of law" that began to gain momentum in the middle of the monarchic period, during the eighth century BCE. Such a process explicitly linked originally profane legal materials, such as the laws (משפטים) found in Exod 21:1–22:29, with the will of Yahweh.[14]

Within the biblical primeval history, after the questioning of divine justice by Cain, the belief in divinely ordained justice is redefined in the double prologue to the flood narrative that follows the listing of Adam's descendants (Gen 5). The sapiential narrator begins by having God state that humans intrinsically pursue things that are damaging to life (Gen 6:5–8). Following this, the Priestly perspective describes Noah, who has already been cast as a new Adam (Gen 5:29),[15] as a צדיק תמים (δίκαιος τέλειος), a completely just person whose communion with God and the

---

12. Sachs, *Gedichte*, 57.

13. See the brief discussion in Dietrich, "Der rote Faden," 18–19, and the detailed discussions in Crüsemann, *Tora*; Otto, *Theologische Ethik*; idem, *Altorientalische und biblische Rechtsgeschichte*.

14. Otto, *Theologische Ethik*, 81–116; Kaiser, *Der Gott des Alten Testaments, Teil 3*, 39–59.

15. This notion is elaborated on in Jewish writings from the Hellenistic and Roman periods, which cast Noah as an archetype of the Messiah; cf. *1 Enoch* 106; and on this, Witte, *Die biblische Urgeschichte*, 201–12, 286; Weigold, "Noah in the Praise," 229–44.

world serves as a standard for what is humanly possible (Gen 6:9, 2 Pet 2:5, cf. Job 1:1).

Based on this triad from the biblical primeval history (the belief in justice, the questioning of justice, and the redefining of justice), which reflects the historical experience of the destruction of the Jerusalem temple in 587 BCE as well as Israel's encounter with Mesopotamian creation myths, three characteristic elements of the biblical conception of divine and human justice can be identified. (1) Divine justice as communion between God and humanity is unpredictable and elusive but can nevertheless be experienced. (2) The human experience of injustice does not preclude communion with God and does not absolve one of the social responsibility to act justly toward others. This focus by Gen 4 on the explicit question of justice is also reflected in the earliest Jewish and Christian reception of the narrative: the Wisdom of Solomon characterizes Cain as the archetype of the unjust person (ἄδικος, Wis 10:3), and in the New Testament Abel serves as the archetype of the just person (δίκαιος, Matt 23:35 par. Luke 11:51, Heb 11:4). At the same time, the story of Cain and Abel points to the destructive potential of unequal economic relations, which within the Old Testament is further criticized in the prophetic books (cf. Isa 5:8–24, Mic 2:1–3), yet without legitimizing violence on the part of the disadvantaged. (3) As the figure of Noah demonstrates, actions and behaviors befitting communion with God and with fellow humans are not impossible but are the exception.

This narrative triad of justice—the establishment, questioning, and redefining of justice—is repeated elsewhere in the Pentateuch, whereby certain aspects are intensified, such as when the key terms for justice (צדק and צדקה/δικαιοσύνη) and judgment (משפט/κρίσις) are used or when individual motifs are developed in which human justice appears or in which divine justice is attributed to humans. The latter case is particularly clear in the literarily and traditio-historically multi-layered Abraham tradition, which in one of its latest stages of development (perhaps originating during the Hellenistic period) describes faith (אמן [*Hiphil*], אמונה/πιστεύω, πίστις) in God as justice (Gen 15:6, Neh 9:8).[16] Within the context of the Pentateuch, this conception reaches its climax in the late Deuteronomistic professions of God's justice (cf. Deut 32:4: צדיק וישר הוא/δίκαιος καὶ ὅσιος κύριος),[17] which constitutes the sole reason for Israel's life and survival (cf. Deut 9:4–6). This late Deuteronomistic conception is further sharpened in the so-called penitential prayer of Daniel (Dan 9:7, 18).

---

16. See Levin, *Der Jahwist*, 174; Köckert, "'Glaube' und 'Gerechtigkeit,'" 415–44.
17. Cf. Neh 9:8; John 17:25; Rom 9:14; 1 John 1:9; Rev 15:3, 16:5.

In describing the relationship between God and his people as a "covenant" (ברית, διαθήκη), which finds its narrative focus in the national foundation myth of Israel's exodus out of Egypt as well as in Deuteronomy (Moses' testament) and which can be traced traditio-historically to ancient Near Eastern contract law and vassal treaties,[18] the Deuteronomistic and Priestly authors who fundamentally shaped the Sinai Pericope (Exod 19:1–Num 10:10) significantly enriched the theological concept of justice in the Old Testament. While the Deuteronomistic use of the term "covenant" emphasizes the aspect of Israel's obligation to obey the laws given by God, which were inserted into the narrative of the theophany at Sinai through a gradual and complex literary and traditio-historical process, the Priestly use of this term emphasizes the commitment that God makes to his people but which also calls for adherence to the cultic and social laws that originated from God. Nevertheless, through its use in both circles of tradition, the concept of "covenant" became a central term in the theological language of justice and law in the Old Testament. Beginning in the Sinai Pericope and in Deuteronomy, where the triad of the establishment, questioning, and redefining of justice is narrated in the giving of the "covenant" (Exod 24:7–8, Deut 9:9–10), its violation (Exod 32, Deut 9:15–29), and its restitution (Exod 34:10, Deut 10:1–8), the term subsequently spread backward and forward both literarily and theologically. Thus, "covenant" appears as a structuring element that interprets the relationship between Yahweh and his people in texts ranging from the Priestly version of the primeval history, ancestral narratives, exodus narrative (Gen 6:18, 9:9, 17:2; Exod 2:24), and Deuteronomistic historiography (1 Kgs 11:11, 2 Kgs 17:1) to (post-)Deuteronomistic reworkings of certain prophetic books (Jer 11) and the Praise of the Fathers in Ben Sira (Sir 44–49).

In deuteronomic-Deuteronomistic literature and in other Old Testament and extracanonical texts influenced by this literature, the term תורה appears as a theological counterweight to the term ברית. Over the course of the literary and theological history of the Old Testament, the term תורה, which originally stood for the teaching or instruction given by a priest, a prophet, or a parent, increasingly took on the meaning of "law" (νόμος), particularly the "law of Yahweh," which, according to the narrative of the Pentateuch, was mediated and written down by Moses (cf. Deut 31:24), before ultimately indicating the books of Genesis to Deuteronomy as a whole—that is, the Torah/ὁ νόμος (Greek Prologue to Ben Sira, 4 Macc

---

18. Cf. Christoph Koch, *Vertrag, Treueid und Bund*.

18:10). Within the context of the Torah piety that developed during the Persian and Hellenistic periods, obedience to the Torah is regarded as a correlate to the "covenant" and is described as justice.[19] Mediated by its translation in the Septuagint (generally with νόμος) and in the Vulgate (generally with *lex*), Christian translations of the Bible up to the present tend to translate the term תורה as "law," which reflects its later use in the Old Testament in a one-sided manner. This also had significant consequences for the history of doctrine and theology and occasionally led to the devaluing of the Old Testament and to Christian anti-Jewish polemics.

3. David and the King as Guarantor of Justice

According to the biblical tradition, David was the founder of a kingdom that united the originally independent tribes of Israel and that at its apex spanned from the Mediterranean Sea to the Euphrates and from Lebanon to Egypt. The greater the time span from the origins of this kingdom, which from an archaeological and literary-historical perspective was a modest Judahite tribal kingdom with sporadic influence over central Palestine,[20] the more David's rule was idealized. This began within the context of Judahite royal ideology during the eighth and seventh centuries BCE, through which the northern kingdom of Israel, which had lost its political autonomy at the hands of the Assyrians in 722 BCE, was to be joined to the south. It is also reflected in the hope of a restoration of the Davidic dynasty following the destruction of the kingdom of Judah by the Babylonians in 587 BCE, which—when such a restoration did not materialize—ultimately developed into the conception of a *David redivivus* or a messianic David during the Persian and Hellenistic periods. Corresponding to the idealization of David, an unknown historian schooled in the book of Deuteronomy noted at the end of the so-called History of David's Rise (1 Sam 16–2 Sam 9):

> So David reigned over all Israel;
> and David administered justice and equity (משפט וצדקה) to all his people. (2 Sam 8:15 par. 1 Chr 18:14)

The conception of the king as the highest judge of his people and as the authority responsible for just social relations, integrated here into the Judahite royal ideology, corresponds to ancient Near Eastern royal ideology

---

19. Deut 33:9–10; Isa 51:7; Ps 78:10, 103:17–18; Ezra 10:3; Tob 14:9; *Ps. Sol.* 10:3–4, 14:2.

20. For a brief overview, see Finkelstein and Silberman, *The Bible Unearthed.*

Fig. 4. Detail of the Susa stela containing the laws of Hammurabi. *ANEP*, 515.

as attested in various forms from Mesopotamia to Egypt and which found its most striking expression in the stela containing the Laws of Hammurabi (LH) from the eighteenth century BCE. The upper portion of this stela (see fig. 4) depicts the Babylonian king Hammurabi standing before the enthroned sun-god Shamash, through whom Hammurabi is to enforce and guarantee law and justice—*kittu* and *mišaru*[21]—on the earth (LH i.27–29):

> . . . at that time, the gods Anu and Enlil, for the enhancement of the well-being of the people, named me by my name: Hammurabi, the pious prince, who venerates the gods, to make justice

---

21. On this word pair, see also Otto, "'Um Gerechtigkeit im Land,'" 109–23.

prevail in the land, to abolish the wicked and the evil, to prevent
the strong from oppressing the weak, to rise the sun-god Shamash
over all humankind, to illuminate the land.[22]

By order of Shamash, the "great judge of heaven and earth,"[23] but also of
Marduk, the patron deity of the city of Babylon,[24] the king upholds law
and justice. The attribution of law and justice to the sun god—whether
the Sumerian god Utu, the Babylonian god Shamash, the Egyptian god
Re (as Amun-Re or Horus-Re), the Hittite god Ishtanush, or the Greek
god Helios[25]—stems from the conception that the sun brings all things
to light.

> Hail to you, Re, perfect each day,
> Who rises at dawn without failing,
> Khepri who wearies himself with toil!
> Your rays are on the face, yet unknown,
> Fine gold does not match your splendor;
> Self-made you fashioned your body,
> Creator uncreated.
> Sole one, unique one, who traverses eternity,
> [Remote one], with millions under his care;
> Your splendor is like heaven's splendor,
> Your color brighter than its hues.
> When you cross the sky all faces see you,
> When you set you are hidden from their sight;
> Daily you give yourself at dawn,
> Safe is your sailing under your majesty.
> In a brief day you race a course,
> Hundred thousands, millions of miles;
> A moment is each day to you,
> It has passed when you go down.
> You also complete the hours of night,
> You order it without pause in your labor.
> Through you do all eyes see,
> They lack aim when your majesty sets.
> When you stir to rise at dawn,

---

22. "The Laws of Hammurabi," trans. Martha Roth (*COS* 2.131:336); cf. Rykle
Borger (*TUAT* 1:40).

23. "The Laws of Hammurabi," lines xlvii.79–xlix.17 (*COS* 2.131:351; *TUAT* 1:
75–77).

24. Cf. "The Laws of Hammurabi," lines v.14–25 (*COS* 2.131:337; *TUAT* 1:44).

25. See also Fauth, *Helios*, 188–94.

Your brightness opens the eyes of the herds;
When you set in the western mountain,
They sleep as in the state of death.[26]

As solar aspects were transferred to the Judahite national deity Yahweh, this conception also found a place in Yahwistic religion (cf. Hos 6:5, Zeph 3:5, Ps 84:12, Mal 3:20).[27] Like Hammurabi, the Egyptian pharaoh, or the Hittite king, the kings of Judah understood themselves as the mediators and guarantors of divine law on the earth.[28] Thus, David is able to speak to his successor Solomon as follows:

> Blessed be the LORD your God, who has delighted in you and set you on the throne of Israel! Because the LORD loved Israel forever, he has made you king to execute justice and righteousness (משפט וצדקה). (1 Kgs 10:9 par. 2 Chr 9:8)

From a sociohistorical perspective, the king's responsibility to practice justice and law toward his people, particularly toward the lowliest members of society, was probably rooted in a pre-monarchic Judahite patronage system—that is, a system of hierarchical, but also familial and personal, connections—that defined justice in terms of loyalty and social solidarity (חסד).[29] Yet, since the just social actions of the king did not follow automatically upon his accession to the throne (cf. 1 Kgs 3:9), the newly enthroned king or a courtly intercessor would pray as follows:

> [1] Give the king your justice (משפטים),[30] O God, and your righteousness (צדקה) to a king's son.
> [2] May he judge (דין) your people with righteousness (צדק), and your poor with justice (משפט).
> [3] May the mountains yield prosperity (שלום) for the people, and the hills, in[31] righteousness (צדקה).

---

26. "First Hymn to the Sun-God" (from a stela of the Brothers Suti and Hor – BM 826), trans. Miriam Lichtheim (*COS* 1.27:43–44); cf. *COS* 1.25; 1.28.

27. For a detailed discussion, see Janowski, "JHWH und der Sonnengott," 192–219; Liwak, "'Sonne der Gerechtigkeit,'" 188–97.

28. Cf. 2 Sam 23:3–4; Prov 16:10–13, 29:14. For corresponding occurrences from Egypt, Mesopotamia, Syria–Palestine, and Anatolia, see, for example, Schmid, *Gerechtigkeit als Weltordnung*, 24–46; Assmann, *Ägypten*, 10–19; Koch, "Ṣädaq," 37–64 (esp. pp. 48–49, 62–63); Maul, "Der assyrische König," 65–77; Niehr, "The Constitutive Principles," 112–30; Schwemer, "Das hethitische Reichspantheon," 241–65.

29. See also Niehr, "The Constitutive Principles," 121–27.

30. The Septuagint and the Peshitta have the singular ("your law").

31. A number of Septuagint, Peshitta, and Vulgate manuscripts omit the preposition, such that "justice" appears as a second object.

[4] May he defend the cause (שָׁפַט) of the poor of the people, give deliverance (יָשַׁע) to the needy, [and crush the oppressor].

[5] May he live[32] while the sun endures, and as long as the moon, throughout all generations.

[6] May he be like rain that falls on the mown grass, like showers that water the earth.

[7] In his days may righteousness[33] flourish and peace abound, until the moon is no more. (Ps 72:1–7)

These verses from Ps 72 have a number of parallels in the Old Testament as well as in the ancient Near Eastern environment of Israel and Judah, from the Old Babylonian period, through the Neo-Assyrian period, and up to the Hellenistic period.[34] Characteristic examples are the biblical texts of Ps 45:7–8 and Isa 11:4, the Phoenician royal inscriptions of Yehimilk of Byblos (mid-tenth century BCE) and of Yehawmilk of Byblos (fifth/fourth century BCE),[35] the coronation hymn for the Assyrian king Assurbanipal (668–631/627 BCE),[36] which is occasionally—albeit incorrectly—regarded as the model for Ps 72,[37] or the songs of praise for the Ptolemaic kings.[38] At the same time, however, the redactional history of Ps 72 also reflects the aforementioned triad of the establishment, questioning, and redefining of justice and applies this to the political conception of justice found in this psalm.

The Old Testament's emphasis on the king's failure to uphold the law and just social relations—and here biblical historiography is particularly critical in comparison to other ancient Near Eastern literature, which resulted from the historical experiences of Israel and Judah, the specific nature of Yahwism, and the literary-sociological background of the Old Testament writings—does not merely reflect actual historical experience. Rather, Yahweh's judgment of the kings of Israel and Judah is founded

---

32. The translation follows the reading of the Septuagint. The Hebrew text has a direct address to God ("they should fear you").

33. Here NRSV follows the Septuagint, where the term δικαιοσύνη "justice" points to the Hebrew term צְדָקָה, which fits better with the parallelism with שָׁלוֹם/εἰρήνη ("peace," cf. v. 3) and is possibly more original than the reading of the MT (צַדִּיק: "the just one").

34. Cf. Liwak, "Der Herrscher als Wohltäter," 163–87 (esp. 168–70); Niehr, "The Constitutive Principles," 112–30; Janowski, "Die Frucht der Gerechtigkeit," 94–134; idem, "Der barmherzige Richter," 85–97.

35. *KAI* 4:6; *KAI* 10:9; and on this, Niehr, "The Constitutive Principles," 115–19, who understands *ṣdq* here as "loyal/loyalty."

36. "Assurbanipal's Coronation Hymn," trans. Alasdair Livingstone (SAA 3 11:26–27).

37. Arneth, *Sonne*.

38. Cf. Callimachus, *Hymn. Jov.* 80–89, as well as Plutarch, *Dem.* 42.8; on the latter, see Weber, *Dichtung und höfische Gesellschaft*, 71–72, 239–40, 412.

upon such failure, calling into question kingship itself in its function of upholding the law.[39] This conception is not based in the putative social structure of an "egalitarian society" in pre-monarchic Israel[40] but rather in the theological reflection of the post-monarchic period, which draws on oracles of judgment in the prophetic literature of the eighth/seventh century BCE (cf. Isa 5:16, 10:22, 28:17–21; Zeph 3:5) and generalizes these in light of a particular theology of history.

Although the Deuteronomistic portrayal of the monarchic period (1 Sam–2 Kgs) portrays the catastrophe of 587 BCE—the fall of the kingdom, the temple, and Judah's political autonomy—as God's ultimately just punishment of Israel, Judah, and their kings, four additional reinterpretations of royal justice are found elsewhere in the Old Testament. These are occasionally referred to as a "divinization" of justice[41] and were developed over the course of the Persian and Hellenistic periods (sixth to fourth centuries BCE) by Priestly and sapiential circles. In this way, the symphony of divine and royal justice appears in different refractions in the Old Testament.

(1) Out of the *eschatologizing* of the older royal ideology arose the conception of a future savior king—a messiah (χριστός)—who would enforce law and justice. Within the Old Testament itself, this can be observed in the messianizing of the royal psalms.[42] By the time of the New Testament at the latest, the term "the just one" (צדיק/δίκαιος) was used as a title for the messiah.[43]

(2) Through a process of *collectivization* and *demo(cra)tization*, the task of guaranteeing the rule of law and enforcing justice in society was transferred from the king to the people (cf. Isa 58).

(3) Related to this process of collectivization is the conception of the just individual who, as an ethical model and mediator of social justice, is endowed with royal traits[44] such that here it is possible to speak of the *individualization* of royal justice. In the transferral of royal conceptions of

---

39. Cf. Jer 22:13–16 (in contrast to 1 Kgs 3:6); Hos 1:4, 3:4, 8:4, 13:10–11; and on this, Liwak, "Der Herrscher als Wohltäter," 179–82.

40. Crüsemann, Widerstand, 194–222.

41. Assmann, *Ägypten*, 11.

42. In addition to Ps 72, cf. Ps 2 and Ps 110 as well as Isa 9:1–6, 11:1–10; Jer 33:15; and Zech 9:9–10; see also Niehr, "The Constitutive Principles," 125, and for a detailed discussion, see Becker, "Psalm 72," 123–40.

43. Matt 27:4 (v.l.), 27:19, Luke 23:47, Acts 3:13–14, 7:52; for a detailed discussion of this see pp. 49, 93–94, 99–100.

44. Cf. Job 29, 31, Ps 1, 119:21, Gen 18:19.

justice to the figure of the suffering servant in the book of Isaiah,[45] both the second and third forms described here are found[46] insofar as the servant can be understood as both an individual and as the representative of a group (the pious of Israel).

(4) The enactment of justice can also be expected directly from the royal deity Yahweh, who will uphold justice at the end of time on a cosmic scale (cf. Isa 45:8), thereby establishing the kingdom of God (מלכות יהוה, βασιλεία τοῦ θεοῦ). This development can be observed, for example, in the eschatologizing of the older kingship-of-Yahweh psalms, which reach far back to the Syro-Palestinian mythology of the Late Bronze Age in their conception of Yahweh's accession to celestial rule following his defeat of the forces of chaos but are transformed during the Persian and Hellenistic periods into songs of Yahweh's eschatological appearance as the judge of nations[47] and represent a *theocratizing* of royal justice. A good example of this phenomenon is found in Ps 97, which contains a traditional core in vv. 1–2 (cf. Ps 89:15, 33:5–6) and an extensive reworking in vv. 3–12.

In this context, the aspect of divine justice as an act of divine salvation and the equating of justice, salvation (שׁלום), trustworthiness (אמונה, אמת), and mercy (חסד), as well as of judging (שׁפט) and saving (יע), appear most clearly, as Bernd Janowski has discussed in particular detail.[48]

> Declare and present your case; let them take counsel together!
> Who told this long ago? Who declared it of old?
> Was it not I, the LORD? There is no other god besides me,
> a righteous God and a Savior;[49] there is no one besides me.
>
> (Isa 45:21)

Finally, a special form of the post-monarchic transformation of the conception of the king as the mediator of the law or lawgiver is the literary

---

45. Isa 42:1–4, 49:1–6, 50:4–9, 52:13–53:12.

46. See also Spieckermann, "Recht und Gerechtigkeit," 264–69, and for a detailed discussion, see the third chapter in this volume, pp. 89, 97–98.

47. Cf. the so-called "oracles against the nations" in Isa 13–23, Jer 46–51, Ezek 25–32, Joel 4, Hab 3.

48. Cf. Hos 2:21, Ps 36:7, 71:15, 72:4, 85:11, 119:142, 144, 160, Dan 9:24; see already Crüsemann, *Gerechtigkeit*, 443–46, and for a detailed discussion, Janowski, "JHWH der Richter," 92–124; idem, *Israel: Der göttliche Richter*, 20–28; idem, *Der barmherzige Richter*, 75–133.

49. Here the LXX uses the epithet Σωτήρ, which was also used for Greek gods and in the Hellenistic ruler cults; cf., for example, Pindar, *Ol.* 5.17 (Zeus), Aeschylus, *Ag.* 512 (Apollo), as well as P.Enteux. 11.6 (Ptolemy IV Philopator), with further occurrences in LSJ s.v. In the NT, the epithet is also applied to Jesus Christ (cf. Luke 2:11). Luther fittingly translated the term as "Heiland" ("redeemer").

Fig. 5. Moses receives the Decalogue (Sarajevo Haggada, ca. 1350). http://historyofinformation.com/images/sarajevo_haggadah-moses_on_sinai.jpg (02/16/2017).

construction of *Moses* as "Israel's lawgiver"—that is, the post-monarchic connection of the legal traditions of Israel and Judah with the pre-monarchic figure of Moses and their incorporation into the presentation of the theophany at Sinai. According to this construct by Deuteronomistic circles, Israel did not receive its fundamental, life-giving laws from a king, as in the aforementioned case of Hammurabi, but instead through Moses, the "man of God" who declares in his literary testament that a king of Israel, if there is to be one (once again), should be a faithful student of Torah (Deut 17:14–20).

4. *Job and the Crisis of Justice*

The most detailed and multifaceted meditation on human and divine justice in the Old Testament is found in the book of Job. Deeply rooted in the ancient Near Eastern discourse on the suffering of the just, which is attested literarily beginning in the third millennium BCE,[50] the book of Job is based on the belief in a just world order provided by the creator-god, who provides a happy life to those who follow the norms of their personal protective deity and of their broader society. The term "just" (צדיק, δίκαιος) applies to those who act in accordance with these norms, such that when used with reference to God—as in the attribute "God-fearing" (ירא אלהים, θεοσεβής)—implies piety, while the term "unjust" can also indicate a lack of piety (cf. Ps 37). In the wisdom literature of ancient Israel as well as of the broader ancient Near East, particularly Egypt, the just person and his or her negative foil, the רשע—which is generally translated as ἀσεβής in the Septuagint and is only translated for practical purposes as "the wicked one" or "the godless one"—embody both a corresponding behavior and the fate that results from such behavior. This belief in a connection between actions and their consequences,[51] which is developed especially in the book of Proverbs through sayings that relate to the most varied areas of human life, is an ethical and religious maxim,[52] and it forms the conceptual point of departure for the book of Job.

Job is the literary figure par excellence for the belief in justice, its questioning, and its redefinition. The figure of Job was conceived of by an unknown poet from the fifth century BCE as someone who upholds the ethical and religious norms of justice in an exemplary fashion, so much so that in Job 1:1 the Septuagint, going beyond the wording of the Hebrew text, explicitly describes him as a δίκαιος, "a just person." Job's suffering serves as a test case for divine and human justice and, indeed, as a test case for the nature of God and humanity (Job 1:6–12, 2:1–8). Over the course of the dialogue between Job, his companions, and God, there is *one* redefinition of justice in particular that must be considered from a theological perspective beyond the boundaries of the book of Job itself. Since neither the explanation for Job's suffering as a test (Job 1:21, 42:12)

---

50. See Sitzler, "Vorwurf gegen Gott;" Uehlinger, "Das Hiob-Buch," 97–163; Sedlmeier, "Ijob," 85–136.

51. On the concept of "connective justice," which in more recent research modifies the term "act-consequence nexus," see the foundational discussion in Assmann, *Ma'at*, 66–67 and the literature cited in n. 6 (p. 29) above.

52. Cf. Prov 10:3, 16, 21; 11:5–6, 19, 31; 12:1–5, 13:6, 14:4, 15:28–29, 20:7, 21:21, 22:8 et al.

nor its interpretation as a didactic lesson (Job 5:17, 36:8–15) nor as a just
punishment for known or unknown wrongdoing (Job 4:7–8, 8:3–4) nor
the reference to the incomprehensible plan of God (Job 38:1–39:30) were
satisfactory to him, an unknown poet, probably during the third century
BCE, inserted the motif of the injustice and sinfulness of humanity as a
function of humanity's created nature at three central points in the book
(Job 25:4; cf. Job 4:17, 15:14):

> How then can a mortal be righteous (יצדק) before God?
> How can one born of woman be pure? (Job 25:4)

The poet's answer is *not at all*—no human can be righteous before God.
In other words, no human can place himself or herself in relation to God
(Job 9:2), whether through excessive piety (Job 1:5) or exemplary social
behavior. Yet neither piety nor ethical behavior toward others (cf. Job
29, 31 as a critical interpretation of the Decalogue)[53] are negated; on the
contrary: based on his religious and moral integrity, Job receives the title
of "servant of God" (Job 1:8, 2:3, 42:7–8), which is reserved for only a
handful of biblical figures. Instead, piety and ethical behavior are relativized. In this way, the correlation between human justice and holiness, between ethics and cultic competency, which can already be seen in the older
cultic liturgies (Pss 15, 24), is redefined. Divine justice as it is defined in
Job 4:17, 15:14, and 25:4, as well as in the traditio-historically and com-
positionally related texts in 1 Kgs 8:46, Ps 143:2, and Qoh 7:20, is the
communion established unilaterally by God with beings who, according
to the later anthropology of the Old Testament, are inclined to sin (חטא/
ἁμαρτάνω; cf. Gen 4:7, Jer 11:23, Ezek 18:21, Ps 51:6–7). According to
the anonymous later editor of the book of Job, this divine communion can
only be initiated by God and can only be accepted by humanity through
a profession of one's own created nature. This concept found linguistic
expression on the one hand in the mythic form of a theophany (Job 38:1,
42:5) and on the other hand in a sapiential saying that is also found in
the literarily and theologically related dialogue between God and Abraham (Gen 18:27)[54] and in the (possibly Essene) songs of praise (*Hodayot*)

---

53. See Witte, "Job in Conversation," 81–100.
54. This is only one of the many parallels between the figures of Job and Abraham that
led to a variety of detailed comparisons between the two figures in rabbinic tradition but also
in patristic literature. A prominent feature of such comparisons is the discussion over whether
Abraham or Job is the more pious figure; see Glatzer, "The God of Job," 41–57; Weinberg,
"Job versus Abraham," 281–96; Jacobs, *The Midrashic Process*, 79–94; Oberhänsli-Widmer,
Hiob in jüdischer Antike, 123–38; Witte, "Hiob und die Väter Israels."

known from Qumran, which are paradigmatic for the self-understanding of the suppliant:

> But now my eye sees you:
> . . . but I am dust and ashes. (Job 42:5–6)[55]

In the final form of the book, it is conceded that Job, for whom the traditional plausibility of the "theonomy" of justice was lost (Job 9:20–22)[56] and who nevertheless professes God's revelation as well as his own creaturely nature, spoke appropriately (נכנה; LXX: ἀληθές "truly," Job 42:7). The righteous sufferer, who ultimately becomes an intercessor for his companions (Job 42:10) and, according to the tradition of a Targum from Qumran dating to the first century BCE, even becomes a propitiatory substitute,[57] thus represents a fourfold recognition: (1) suffering is not a sign of divine absence; (2) there can be innocent suffering; (3) divine justice can elude human standards but not humanity itself; and (4) the suffering of the just can have the function of strengthening communities. The last of these is developed in the conception of the suffering servant in the book of Isaiah (cf. Isa 52:13–53:12) and is reinterpreted in the Christology of the New Testament (cf. Mark 10:45).[58] That is, a just person who suffers learns from the unjust treatment by God—and none of the literary layers of the book of Job, including the so-called heavenly scenes which introduce the *satan* as a divine dialogue partner (cf. Job 2:3), leave any doubt that God is the source of Job's suffering—that human justice is based solely in God's relationship to humanity (Job 33:23–26, cf. 1QS X, 11, XI, 3, 12–14). In this respect, Job, like his Qumranic relatives, anticipates the Pauline conception of divine justice and the justification of the sinner. Here it should be emphasized, however, that in the Old Testament as a whole, the concept of justification, which is so central to Christian theology, appears only rarely and belongs to later literary layers, whereby the Greek translation, especially in the Psalms (cf. Ps 72:13 LXX, Ps 142:2 LXX), reflects a characteristic development in the direction of the New Testament's understanding of justification.[59]

---

55. Cf. 1QHᵃ IX, 21–26; XI, 23–24; XV, 28–29; XVII, 13–18; XVIII, 3–7; 1QS XI, 9–10; on the translation of על־עפר ואפר proposed above, see Witte, *Vom Leiden zur Lehre*, 200–204.

56. Spieckermann, "Recht und Gerechtigkeit," 272–73.

57. Cf. 11QtgJob XXXVIII, 3 (García Martínez and Tigchelaar, *The Dead Sea Scrolls*, vol. 2, 1200–1201).

58. From the vast amount of literature on this motif, see esp. Janowski and Stuhlmacher, *Der leidende Gottesknecht*.

59. See Spieckermann, "Rechtfertigung I," 282–85.

The pattern of thought traced in the poetry of the book of Job is not limited to the latter, even if it is expressed there in a unique literary and theological manner, but rather has left a number of traces in the Old Testament, generally in poetic texts that originated through the reflection of Jewish sages on divine justice and human justice during the Persian and especially the Hellenistic period,[60] such as in Ps 51, Ps 143, Lam 3, or, beyond the boundaries of the canon, *Psalm of Solomon* 3 and 1QHodayot.

5. *The Torah of Habakkuk*

As a prophetic voice within the Old Testament's discourse on justice, rather than one of the larger prophetic books (Isaiah, Jeremiah, Ezekiel), here the book of Habakkuk will be discussed in light of its unique mixture of conceptions of justice from the legal, prophetic, cultic, and sapiential traditions, as well as in light of its prominent history of reception. Corresponding to its literary placement within the Book of the Twelve, the book of Habakkuk has its narrative setting in the seventh century BCE, but in light of its reworked traditions and theological themes, it can be understood as a proto-apocalyptic text from the fourth/third century BCE.[61]

In the compositional and thematic center of the book of Habakkuk is the statement "But the righteous person lives by his [or her] faith/trust (אמונתו)," which came to be of fundamental importance to the Pauline— and later, to the Lutheran—conception of justification (Hab 2:4). Embedded within a prophetic vision, this statement is by no means an everyday proverb.[62] Rather, it is a redefinition of the relationship between God and humanity. This can be seen in the compositional and traditio-historical structure of the book of Habakkuk, which, in light of its superscription in Hab 1:1 and the command to write in 2:2, emerges as a vision report. In this vision, the prophet first sees the breakdown of justice in his own community, which is reflected in the prevalence of violence (חמס, described in Gen 6:13 as the catalyst for the flood), the laxness of Torah observance, and the mistreatment of the just by the wicked (Hab 1:2–4). Then the prophet witnesses the rise of a foreign people that conquers the world and regards itself as God (Hab 1:5–17). This prompts the prophet to repeated lamentations and entreaties before God, requesting a demonstration of God's justice (Hab 1:12–13, 2:1–5), before he hears the nations of the world intoning woes over the world power that had defied all social, reli-

---

60. See Jeremias, *Gerechtigkeit und Leben.*
61. For this literary-historical evaluation, see Witte, "Orakel und Gebete."
62. Wellhausen, *Die kleinen Propheten*, 168.

gious, and moral norms (Hab 2:6–20)[63] and finally sees Yahweh take the stage of world history, enacting his judicial power (Hab 3:1–19).

What began as a lament to and against Yahweh thus ends as a profession of trust in Yahweh. Characteristic of the book is how it accounts for the survival of the just through the reception of pentateuchal traditions, such as the writing of divine revelation on tablets (cf. Deut 1:5, 27:8) and Yahweh's emergence from Teman and Paran to enact justice (cf. Deut 33:2)—namely, through belief in the judgment-theophany witnessed by Habakkuk.[64] Here, the prophetic vision emerges alongside the Torah of Moses, which gives life to those who observe its commandments (Deut 30:19), as the object of life-sustaining belief. The notion that obedience to the Torah gives life, which is particularly prominent in the book of Deuteronomy, had a strong influence in early Judaism (cf. Ps 119:142–144, Sir 17:11 LXX, 45:5, *Pss. Sol.* 9:5) and also underlies the saying in tractate *Avot* of the Mishnah, "One who increases Torah, increases life" (*m. Avot* 2.8). Nevertheless, this notion was subjected to an inner-biblical critique, which in the Old Testament finds its strongest expression in Jer 31:31–34 and in the concept of a "new heart" (Ezek 36:26) and in the New Testament is transformed by the theology of Paul, in which the human ability to fulfill the divine demand to practice justice (Mic 6:8) is made dependent upon a fundamental re-creation of humanity (2 Cor 5:16–21).

With Hab 2:4, the Mosaic Torah is not abrogated but is instead supplemented by the prophetic Torah. Postbiblical Judaism recognized the connections between the vision of Habakkuk and the Torah of Moses, as can be seen in the saying in the Babylonian Talmud that through Hab 2:4 Habakkuk boiled down the 613 Mosaic commandments into *one* commandment (*b. Mak.* 24a). However, against this rabbinic tradition, which reflects the notion (also rightly observed in recent critical scholarship) that the prophets are interpreters of the Torah, it should be emphasized that Hab 2:4 is less a witness to the identity of the prophetic mission with the Torah than to the critical discourse over the contents, shape, and authority of the Mosaic Torah within Judaism during the Persian and Hellenistic periods.[65] Regarding the concept of justice, it is noteworthy that in the case of Habakkuk, divine justice is enacted through a worldwide judgment of cosmic dimensions,[66] while human justice is articulated through belief in the divine acts of justice seen by the prophet.

---

63. Cf. corresponding oracles of woe in Isa 5:8–24, Jer 22:13–17, Mic 2:1 et al.

64. For a detailed discussion of this cf. Witte, "Orakel und Gebete," 67–91.

65. On this, see Knoppers and Levinson, *The Pentateuch as Torah*; Schipper and Teeter, *Wisdom and Torah*.

66. Cf. Joel 4; Zech 14; Dan 2, 7; Jer 25; Ps 9:20.

Already in antiquity, the reading of Hab 2:4 presented here—which in my view also reflects the intention of the text's author—was not the only possible interpretation, as is shown by a well-known commentary (*pesher*) on the book of Habakkuk from Qumran dating to the first century BCE. This commentary identifies the just with all of the "doers of the Torah in the house of Judah," whom God will save from the eschatological judgment "on account of their belief (or trust) in the Teacher of Righteousness," the founder of the Qumran community (1QpHab VIII, 1–3).[67] Paul interprets Hab 2:4 in yet another way, due not least to a slight difference between the Greek and Hebrew versions of the verse (Rom 1:17).[68]

6. *Pseudo-Solomon's Promotion of Justice*

The Wisdom of Solomon, which probably originated in the early Roman imperial period in the metropolis of Alexandria and is thus the latest book in the Old Testament, begins in the style of a royal didactic text with an invocation to the rulers of the world to love justice (Wis 1:1) before then developing a rhetorically sophisticated treatise on justice in general. In this text, the anonymous author, who was educated in both Jewish scriptures and in Hellenistic Greek literature and philosophy and—like Qohelet, who also wrote on the issue of justice during the Hellenistic period (cf. Qoh 1:6, 5:7, 7:15)—was identified in postbiblical tradition with Solomon on the basis of the allusions to 1 Kgs 3:6–9 and 1 Kgs 8–10 in Wis 6:24–25, 7:1, 9:1–18, combined pagan and Jewish concepts in a unique way.

In defining justice (δικαιοσύνη) as one of the cardinal virtues (ἀρετή) alongside self-control (σωφροσύνη), understanding (φρόνησις), and courage (ἀνδρεία), the author of the Wisdom of Solomon was following the classical path of Greek philosophy that had been tread from the time of Plato up to the Hellenistic-Roman ethics of courage (Wis 8:7). At the same time, however, he drew on his Jewish heritage in placing justice in parallel with reflection on God and the search for God—that is, with the will to be in communion with God (Wis 1:1)—or in understanding justice as fundamental to the nature of the *one* God of Israel who acts power-

---

67. Translation from García Martínez and Tigchelaar, *Dead Sea Scrolls*, vol. 1, 16–17.

68. Thus, Paul reads "from (as a result of) faith/trust (πίστις)" without the possessive pronoun. In Hab 2:4, instead of the third-person singular possessive suffix in the Masoretic Text, the Septuagint has a first-person singular possessive pronoun with reference to God (πίστις μου), which can be translated as either a subjective genitive ("from [as a result of] my faith/trust") or an objective genitive ("from [as a result of] faith/trust in me").

fully in creation and history (Wis 12:16–17).[69] The description of the pious—that is, those who observe the Torah and its norms in the Diaspora
(Wis 2:12–13)—and of Israel's ancestors from the biblical narratives as
just (δίκαιοι) and as guided and protected by divine wisdom (Wis 10) is
also based on the use of the term "just" in Hebrew texts from the Persian
and Hellenistic periods.[70]

What is innovative is the combination of the conceptions of justice
and immortality. Here, the Alexandrian thinker redefines divine justice,
which has been called into question by an evidently contemporary persecution of the just, through a double eschatological perspective. (1) If
one loses one's life for the sake of one's justice—one's faithfulness to God
and Torah (Wis 2:12–13, cf. Isa 52:13–53:12)—then this is only to attain an even more intense communion with God *after death*, since, as Wis
3:1 formulates in an extension of Ps 49:16,[71] "the souls of the righteous
are in the hand of God, and no torment will ever touch them" (cf. Wis
4:7, 5:15). (2) Justice in the sense of communion with God is immortal
(ἀθάνατος, Wis 1:15), as it is realized through the knowledge of God and
through immortality (ἀθανασία, Wis 15:3).

With this interplay of knowledge of God, justice, and immortality,
the anonymous author of the Wisdom of Solomon, whom Martin Luther
and others with good reason compared with the Jewish philosopher Philo
of Alexandria,[72] moved within an intellectual milieu that is comparable
to that of the Gospel of John (cf. Wis 15:3, John 17:3). The Wisdom of
Solomon also shares with the Gospel of John the notion that the justice of
God will be revealed in the eschatological glorification of God's followers
(cf. Wis 19:22, John 17:1, 5).

7. Conclusion

Old Testament theology is a philological enterprise. As such, regarding the theme of justice, it involves the meaning and use of the Hebrew
terms for justice and law (מישור, משפט, צדקה, צדק) and their Greek equivalents in the Septuagint (δίκη, δικαιοσύνη, κρίσις, κρίμα, etc.).[73]

---

69. Cf. Jer 32:17–20, Sir 18:1–2.
70. See also the reference to Jesus as the exemplary just person (δίκαιος) in Luke 23:47.
71. See Witte, "'Aber Gott wird meine Seele erlösen,'" 67–93. On the post-mortem
resolution of the problem of justice, see also Dan 12:1–3 and 2 Macc 7:9.
72. Cf. Luther, "Vorrede auff die Weisheit," 1699.
73. The term θέμις ("custom/law/legislation"), which was important in pagan Greek
law and was mythically personified as Themis, daughter of Uranus and Gē/Gaia and mother
(with Zeus as the father) of the Hours, of Dike, Eunomia, and Eirene (cf. Hesiod, *Theog.*

Old Testament theology is a historical enterprise. As such, it contributes to biblical theology in the form of the history of religion, literary history, and reception history. Regarding the subject at hand, this means that Old Testament theology, within the framework of biblical theology, explains (1) the nature and origins of both ancient Near Eastern and Hellenistic Greek conceptions of justice as expressed in their Israelite-Jewish forms; (2) the literary forms and contexts of Israelite-Jewish conceptions of justice spanning from cultic poetry, sapiential sayings, and prophetic words of judgment to quasi-philosophical treatises and theological narratives; and (3) the inner-biblical development of conceptions of justice and their extrabiblical reception in art and literature. For the latter, reference should once again be made to the inner-biblical discourse on the justice of God in the different literary layers of Genesis, Job, Qohelet, and Ben Sira as well as to the reception of the Job theme in modern literature.[74]

Old Testament theology is an aesthetic enterprise. As such, it contributes to biblical theology regarding the subject of justice by showing how and in what form Old Testament texts evoke images of justice for readers or listeners, how individual conceptions of justice arise and take shape in the process of reading and hearing these texts, and how readers and listeners participate in the biblical discourse on justice, whether they reach their own answer regarding divine justice through their reading of the book of Job, whether they feel challenged to act justly through the prophetic warning to "Maintain justice, and do what is right" (Isa 56:1), or whether they join in the profession of the Psalmist, "You are righteous, O LORD" (Ps 119:137).

Old Testament theology is an essential part of biblical theology. As such, it is not its task to explain how, for example, Paul read Gen 15:6, Hab 2:4, or the book of Job (these are the task of New Testament scholarship) but rather to bring to light the historical, religious, and theological impulses and contexts that produced these texts and how they speak about divine and human justice. Old Testament theology thus presents the Old Testament's descriptions of justice, which should be investigated both in terms of how they gave meaning and structure to peoples' lives at the time they were written *and* how they can do the same in the present. Regarding the topic of justice in particular, Old Testament theology can display its inner-biblical critical potential, such as by showing that the Pauline understanding of Hab 2:4 is not the only one—which can already be seen in the contrasting interpretations of the commentary on Habakkuk from

135, 901–2), only appears in the LXX in 2 Macc 6:20 and 12:14 in the expression "it is just/equitable," while the New Testament authors do not use the term at all.

74. Oberhänsli-Widmer, *Hiob in jüdischer Antike*; Langenhorst, *Hiob unser Zeitgenosse*.

Qumran (1QpHab), the epistle to the Romans, and the epistle of James—
or by thematizing aspects of justice that either do not appear at all in the
New Testament or only appear in a restrained manner, such as the cosmic
dimension of justice as timeless rules for life that were embedded in the
world by the creator-god, a notion that ultimately has its origins in the
ancient Near East and ancient Egypt but was also part of Classical Greek
thought.[75]

Inasmuch as justice in the Old Testament always describes a relationship connected to God, established by God, and also shaped by God at the
level of human interaction,[76] there is ultimately only *one* conception of justice in the Old Testament, regardless of the different traditio- and literary-
historical backgrounds of the biblical texts that address this topic.[77] Just as
the starting point for the theological and anthropological fulfillment and
implementation of δικαιοσύνη in the New Testament is salvation through
Jesus Christ,[78] in the Old Testament, God is likewise the starting point,
the point of reference, and the goal of justice, as the example of the Decalogue demonstrates. What we can distinguish in the *one* conception of
justice in the Old Testament—and this is particularly generative for a correlation with the New Testament, but also with extra-biblical religious and
philosophical concepts—are different dimensions, problematizations, and
reinterpretations of justice; in other words: questions such as on which
theological and anthropological levels justice is thematized, how justice
is questioned, how this is articulated, and how justice is redefined such
that it can be attributed to God and to humans. This includes exposing
the potential for giving meaning to life, which has no future without a
stable relationship between God and humanity, among humanity itself,
and between humanity and the environment—that is, without justice in
its vertical and horizontal dimensions.

Old Testament theology is an applied form of inquiry. Regarding the
theme of justice, this means that Old Testament theology, when combined

---

75. Cf. on this the classic foundational work of Schmid, *Gerechtigkeit als Weltordnung*,
23–66, with corresponding examples for the ancient Near East and ancient Egypt, and for
a brief treatment, Niehr, "The Constitutive Principles," 122–23. Within Greek literature,
further reference could be made to Hesiod, *Op.* 218–28, 255–84; Aeschylus, *Cho.* 639, 946;
Sophocles, *Oed. col.* 1381; *Ant.* 451; on this, see Kaiser, "Dike und Sedaqa," 1–23.

76. See already Hempel, "Gottesgedanke und Rechtsgestaltung," 377–95; and Horst,
"Gerechtigkeit Gottes," 1403–6, as well as, more recently, Spieckermann, "Recht und Gerechtigkeit," 255.

77. For a different approach, see, for example, Janowski, "Israel: Der göttliche Richter," 20–28, who speaks of three conceptions of justice but subsequently (and more fittingly)
differentiates between three different yet connected levels of the discourse of justice: the
religious level, the political-social level, and the anthropological level (ibid., 21).

78. Lührmann, *Gerechtigkeit*, 419.

with New Testament theology, critically reflects conceptions of justice in the Church and in society[79] and calls for justice in the name of God, whom both the Old and New Testaments profess as the *single* Lord of creation and history and thus as the Lord of all aspects of life. Here, the sapiential saying that "righteousness exalts a nation" (Prov 14:34), the late prophetic emphasis on individual responsibility before God with its sharp dialectic between sin (חטא) and justice in Ezek 18, or the opening invocation of the Wisdom of Solomon, which calls for those in the world with political and economic influence to love justice (Wis 1:1), are of both enduring and—in light of the economic and social problems associated with globalization—immediate relevance.

---

79. Cf. Dietrich, "Der rote Faden," 28.

CHAPTER 3

From Yahweh to the Messiah:

Images of God in the Old Testament as Background for the Discourse on Jesus Christ in the New Testament

> Long ago God spoke to our ancestors in many and various ways
> by the prophets, but in these last days he has spoken to us by a
> Son, whom he appointed heir of all things, through whom he
> also created the worlds. — Heb 1:1–2

1. Introduction

The theological question of Jesus Christ requires a presentation of the theology (or theologies) of the Old Testament in three respects.

First: The New Testament authors explained the life, death, and resurrection of Jesus—which they regarded as the definitive revelation of God—in light of the sacred scriptures of early Judaism, which only came to be regarded as the Old Testament with the development of a collection of New Testament scriptures within the Church, as well as in light of additional Jewish writings that did not become canonical, and by means of Old Testament images, motifs, and concepts.

Second: Jesus himself read and interpreted the sacred scriptures that would later be called the "Old Testament."

Third: The theology of the Old Testament as a historical and systematic discipline reflects the discourse on God in the Old Testament against its historical background and, in the context of Christian theology, relates to the discourse on God in the New Testament. The last aspect results from the fact that the New Testament draws on the religious language and thought of the Old Testament and represents a continuation of the latter in terms of literary history. For the New Testament authors, the God who is accessible in the person of Jesus is identical to the God to whom the Old

53

Testament bears witness, and Jesus is the eschatological savior expected in the Old Testament, to whom the New Testament authors (at the latest) gave the title "Messiah/Christ," which was also used in Judaism during the same period to designate an eschatological savior and deliverer. Finally, early Christianity, which adopted the sacred scriptures of early Judaism, understood itself both in continuity and discontinuity with biblical Israel as representing the (new) people of God. Yet if Jesus Christ is understood as the definitive revelation of God, then within the context of Christian theology, the discourse on God in the Old Testament ultimately becomes part of Christology.[1]

The use of scripture by Jesus and by the New Testament authors is part of the history of reception and thus falls within the realm of New Testament scholarship as well as dogmatics and church history. In contrast, describing the relationship between the discourse on God in the Old and New Testaments is a legitimate part of Old Testament theology in the sense of a religio-historical classification of the ways of experiencing God articulated in the Old Testament, including their reception in New Testament texts relating to Jesus Christ. Moreover, describing this relationship is a substantial part of biblical theology, as it highlights fundamental anthropological and theological themes in both testaments in terms of their historical and topical similarities and differences.

2. Jesus Christ as the Subject of Old Testament Exegesis

Regardless of the question whether Jesus' use of Israel's scriptures in the New Testament goes back to Jesus himself or is the result of the post-resurrection reflection on the figure of Jesus as the Messiah/Christ, it is well known that three basic approaches to the use of scripture can be observed in the New Testament: allegorical, typological, and eschatological. During the Hellenistic and Roman periods, these three types of interpretation were hardly limited to the correlation of Old Testament texts with Jesus Christ or to Christian hermeneutics more broadly. They were also applied to other biblical topics and were widespread in both early Judaism and in antique pagan thought, and to a certain extent have their roots in the latter. Underlying all three approaches is the desire to reveal the contemporary meaning of a text that is regarded as normative yet whose relevance for the present is either not immediately apparent or which has been radically questioned by a new historical experience. Within the context of the New Testament, these three approaches work in two directions: on

---

1. Cf. Gese, "Erwägungen zur Einheit," 30.

the one hand they seek to interpret the scriptures of Israel in light of the experience of Jesus Christ, and on the other hand they themselves serve to explain the experience of Jesus Christ.

2.1. Jesus Christ as Reflected in the Allegorical Interpretation of the Old Testament

Allegorical interpretation is based on the notion that a text possesses a deeper (allegorical) meaning that goes beyond its literal meaning, and that the allegorical meaning can be extracted by decoding the text's constituent parts (e.g., words, phrases, etymologies, numbers, and grammatical phenomena). Accordingly, allegorical interpretation differentiates between the surface level of a text and its deeper dimension, which must first be deciphered. In the view of the allegorical interpreter, the latter represents the true meaning of the text. Inasmuch as allegories are found within both the Old and New Testaments themselves (cf. Isa 5:1–7, Ezek 34, and John 10:1–18), allegorical interpretation has an immediate point of contact within the Bible itself. Nevertheless, early Christian allegorical interpretation is historically linked to the hermeneutics of the Hellenistic Jewish Diaspora, particularly the works of Philo of Alexandria (25 BCE–ca. 50 CE), which in turn reflects the pagan interpretation of Homer and of Greek mythology since the sixth/fifth century BCE.

Referring to Jesus Christ, Gal 4:21–31 offers a typical (and particularly complex) example of the allegorical interpretation of scripture (cf. Gal 4:24). Here, Paul relates the narratives of Abraham, his wife Sarah, their maidservant Hagar, and the sons born to each of these women, Isaac and Ishmael (Genesis 16, 21), to the relationship between the way to God connected to the "law" (νόμος, תורה, *lex*) and the salvation made possible through faith (πίστις, אמונה, *fides*) in Jesus Christ. In doing so, Paul uses an idiosyncratic Arabian etymology to interpret the maidservant Hagar as a cipher for Mount Sinai (located in Arabia),[2] where according to Exod 19 the Torah was revealed, while in Sarah, the free woman, he sees the mother of the promised son (Gen 18:10), the son who is free from the "law." Correspondingly, Isaac appears as a cipher for Jesus Christ and for those who believe in him. A correlation between Isaac and Jesus Christ is also found elsewhere in the New Testament (Rom 9:7; Heb 11:8–9, 17–19), and the narrative of the binding of Isaac (Gen 22:1–19) left a deep trace already in early Christian art.[3]

---

2. Gese, "Τὸ δὲ Ἁγὰρ Σινὰ," 59–61.
3. Lucchesi Palli, "Abraham," 23–30; Altripp, "Isaac (Patriarch)," 281.

2.2. Jesus Christ as Reflected in the Typological Interpretation
   of the Old Testament

Typological interpretation represents a specific form of allegorical interpretation. According to this interpretive approach, particular figures or events in the past appear as forerunners (τύποι, cf. Rom 5:14) of later figures or events. In contrast to allegorical interpretation, in the typological reading of a text the figures or events that are brought together are not identified with each other but instead understood as structural equivalents.

There is a typological interpretation oriented toward the New Testament for almost every major figure and event that plays an important role in the Old Testament's representation of the history of Israel. For example, Adam, the ancestors, Moses, David, Solomon, and Elijah, as well as the exodus and the divine support for Israel during the wilderness journey were understood as foreshadowings of Jesus Christ or of God's acting through Jesus Christ and were also drawn upon in interpreting Jesus' life, death, and resurrection. Here, specific functions of individual biblical figures or particular structures of events are read typologically with reference to Jesus Christ, such as the universal consequences of Adam's sin,[4] the liberating acts of God in the exodus,[5] the deliverance of Israel in the wilderness by Moses,[6] or the wisdom of Solomon.[7]

The epistle to the Hebrews offers a particularly developed typology in its reference to the figure of Melchizedek from Gen 14:18–22 and Ps 110:4 (which is dependent on the former), who is understood as the model high priest and as a prototype for Jesus Christ in his role as priest.[8] In this way, the Melchizedek typology in the epistle to the Hebrews demonstrates how early Christian authors took part in a widespread exegetical discourse—which is also reflected in the speculations on Melchizedek known from the Qumran texts (11Q13)[9]—and how they drew on cultic concepts from early Judaism (temple, priests, sacrifice, expiation)[10] in interpreting the person and work of Jesus Christ.

---

4. Rom 5:14 with reference to Gen 2–3.
5. Matt 2:15, citing Hos 11:1; see also 1 Cor 10:1–4, with an allegorical interpretation of Exod 17:6.
6. Cf. John 3:14–16 with Num 21:4–9.
7. Cf. Matt 12:42 par. Luke 11:31; on this, see Oeming, "Salomo-Christologie."
8. Cf. Heb 2:17, 5:5–10, 6:20, 7:11–17, 8:1–6, 9:11.
9. On this, see Fabry and Scholtissek, *Der Messias*, 49–50; von Nordheim, *Geboren von der Morgenröte*, 240–67.
10. See §4.5 below (pp. 86ff.).

2.3. *Jesus Christ as Reflected in the Eschatological Interpretation of the Old Testament*

The most important hermeneutical approach both for Jesus' use of scripture and that of the New Testament authors is the eschatological interpretation of Israel's scriptures. In an eschatological reading, texts are understood as prophecies about the end times (τὰ ἔσχατα). In this respect, eschatological exegesis is not limited to the interpretation of texts oriented toward the future, such as prophetic oracles, but can also extend to texts concerned with the present, such as sapiential admonitions or prayers of lamentation or supplication. Moreover, an eschatological hermeneutic is not specifically Christian; rather, an eschatological *relecture* of older texts is already found within the scriptures of Israel by the fourth/third century BCE at the latest, such as in the narrative books.[11] Likewise, the prophetic books were reworked into a two- or three-part universal eschatological drama leading in stages from judgment upon Israel to judgment on the nations and on the entire world and finally to ultimate salvation brought about by God. Older Yahweh-is-king psalms (Pss 29, 47, 93, 96–99) were transformed into songs of God's eschatological kingship, and individual wisdom texts (cf. Ps 37, Prov 2) were eschatologized. Around the same time as Jesus' life and ministry, well-known Jewish commentaries from Qumran on individual prophetic books and psalms (*pesharim*) likewise attest to an eschatological interpretation of scripture.[12] Finally, an eschatological understanding of traditional texts can also be seen in the pagan culture of the Hellenistic and Roman periods.[13]

Two aspects characterize the eschatological understanding found in the New Testament. First, Jesus himself explained his person and ministry with metaphors that are connected to the end times in the scriptures of Israel. This applies to the conception of the advent of God's ultimate kingship (מלכות יהוה / βασιλεία τοῦ θεοῦ), which is expressed especially in the prophetic books, in individual psalms, and in the apocalyptic passages of the book of Daniel,[14] and it also applies to the title of "son of man" (בן אדם, בר נש / υἱὸς τοῦ ἀνθρώπου) found especially in the early Jewish apocalyptic writings, which ultimately did not enter the canon of scripture. The development of the latter and its use in the Old Testament spans

---

11. Cf. Gen 49:8–12*, Num 24:15–24*, 1 Sam 2:1–10*.

12. Cf. 1QpHab, 1QpNah, or 4Q171.

13. Cf. the Egyptian texts "The Lamb of Bocchoris" and the "Potter's Oracle" (Quack, *Einführung in die altägyptische Literaturgeschichte III*, 176–81; Collins, *The Apocalyptic Imagination*, 36–37, 118, 121).

14. Cf. Isa 24:23; Mic 4:7; Zech 14:17; Pss 96–99, 145–46; Dan 7:27.

from the simple reference to a human being in relation to God (Ps 8:5), to the specific title given to the prophet Ezekiel[15] and to the title of an ambiguous, eschatological, and celestial (savior) figure (Dan 7:13).[16] Second, early Christian authors, albeit with characteristic differences in their understanding of eschatology, interpreted the life, death, and resurrection of Jesus as a fulfillment of "Old Testament" prophecies. Just as the various Old Testament eschatologies revolve around the definitive action of the one and only God Yahweh, the New Testament authors saw in Jesus Christ the irreversible and unsurpassable acts of God's salvation.

Correspondingly, a characteristic feature of the reception of Old Testament scriptures in the New Testament is *the eschatological fulfillment of prophecy*, according to which Jesus is identified with different eschatological savior figures anticipated in early Judaism, and the decisive events in his life, from his birth to his death on the cross and resurrection, are interpreted as God's actions in fulfillment of scripture.[17] In this way, the fulfillment of prophecy attributed to Jesus Christ can relate both to the explicit citation of individual passages of scripture as well as to the entire collection of Israel's sacred scriptures, which consisted of the *Torah*, the *Nevi'im*, and the (still developing) *Ketuvim*. Thus, for example, Luke presents the resurrected Christ as an exemplary interpreter of Israel's scriptures (Luke 24:27), and other New Testament texts also speak of such a reading of the scriptures of Israel that was first made possible by Jesus Christ (Acts 8:26–40, 2 Cor 3:12–18).

Within the context of eschatological interpretation, the New Testament authors occasionally set up an antithesis between Jesus Christ, who is understood as the definitive revelation of God, and God's prior revelations to Abraham and Moses as recorded in the Torah, which are then regarded as provisional or obsolete. In this case, Jesus Christ does not primarily fulfill but rather surpasses Old Testament conceptions of salvation. In this way, the Old Testament becomes a contrast to the life and ministry of Jesus Christ.[18] In terms of its structure, such an understanding of scripture is not uniquely Christian, as can be seen in the critique of the Torah of Moses or one's approach to it by certain sapiential and prophetic authors within the Old Testament itself,[19] in esoteric texts from Qumran,[20] or in

---

15. Ezek 2:1 and 93 additional occurrences in Ezekiel.

16. Cf. *1 Enoch* 46:1–6, *4 Ezra* 13:3–4.

17. Cf. Matt 2:5–6 with Mic 5:1; Acts 8:30–36 with Isa 53:7–8; and 1 Cor 15:3–4 with Isa 53:4–5, Hos 6:2, Ps 16:8–11.

18. Cf. John 1:17, 7:23, 8:17–18, 10:34–36; Rom 3:21–22; Gal 2:21; Heb 3:1–6.

19. Cf. Job 31 (and on this, Witte, "Does the Torah," 54–65) and Jer 31 (and on this, Levin, *Die Verheißung des neuen Bundes*, 132–46, 257–64), respectively.

20. Cf. 1Q26/4Q415–418; and on this, Goff, *Discerning Wisdom*, 9–67.

the early Jewish Enoch tradition,[21] although it took on a new quality in its exclusive connection to Jesus Christ. Even more clearly than in the allegorical and typological modes of interpretation, the eschatological fulfillment of prophecy and its antithetical variant demonstrate the mutual influence between the interpretation of the Old Testament in light of Jesus Christ and the interpretation of the person and ministry of Jesus in light of the Old Testament.

2.4. Jesus Christ as Reflected in the Historical-Critical Interpretation of the Old Testament

In its basic structure and hermeneutical approach, the focus on Jesus Christ in the context of Old Testament interpretation outlined above spans from the early Church through the Middle Ages and Martin Luther (1483–1546) up to certain decidedly christological or christocentric interpretations in the twentieth century, such as the works of Otto Procksch (1874–1947) and especially Wilhelm Vischer (1895–1988).[22] The opening sentences of Otto Procksch's *Theologie des Alten Testaments* and of the first volume of Wilhelm Vischer's *Christuszeugnis des Alten Testaments* illustrate their approach:

> All theology is Christology. Jesus Christ is the only figure in the world we perceive in which God's revelation is complete. God is in Christ and Christ in God; this relationship between God and humanity is completely unique in history; it will not be repeated in any other form.[23]

> The Old Testament says what the Christ is, while the New Testament says who he is, such that this is clear: only the one who recognizes Jesus as the Christ knows Jesus, and only the one who knows what the Christ is knows that Jesus is the Christ. Thus, both Testaments, inspired by a single Spirit, point to each other [. . .].[24]

---

21. See Bedenbender, "Mose," 182–203.

22. See Preuß, *Das Alte Testament*, 85–94, and Reimer, "Old Testament Christology," 380–400; for a detailed discussion of Vischer, see also Felber, *Wilhelm Vischer*.

23. "Alle Theologie ist Christologie. Jesus Christus ist die einzige Gestalt unserer Erfahrungswelt, in der Gottes Offenbarung vollständig ist. Gott ist in Christus und Christus in Gott, dies Verhältnis zwischen Gott und Mensch ist völlig einzigartig in der Geschichte; es wiederholt sich in keiner andern Gestalt" (Procksch, *Theologie*, 1).

24. "Das Alte Testament sagt, was der Christus ist, das Neue, wer er ist, und zwar so, daß deutlich wird: nur der kennt Jesus, der ihn als den Christus erkennt, und nur der weiß, was der Christus ist, der weiß, daß er Jesus ist. So deuten die beiden Testamente, von Einem Geiste durchhaucht, gegenseitig aufeinander [. . .]." (Vischer, *Das Christuszeugnis* [6th ed.; 1943], 7).

Following Enlightenment philosophy and Romanticism, historical-critical biblical scholarship, which emerged in the seventeenth/eighteenth centuries, inquired into the original historical situation and intention as well as the first addressees of a text. With its rise, the allegorical, typological, and eschatological (and occasionally also the Christological) interpretations of the Old Testament were problematized to varying degrees and criticized as highly selective ways of explaining the text that were not derived from the Old Testament texts themselves and sometimes departed significantly from the original meaning of the text.[25] In light of the real hermeneutical deficiencies of allegorical, typological, and eschatological interpretation and influenced by the conditions of historical thinking, present-day Christian theology faces the challenge of presenting Jesus Christ as the subject not only of the New Testament but also of the Old Testament. If Christian theology forfeits this task, then either the traditio- and literary-historical as well as thematic connection between the two Testaments will be dissolved and the investigation of the texts found in the Old Testament will be delegated to the historical study of ancient Near Eastern and classical literature and religion, as was the case with the Old Testament scholar and the founder of modern Assyriology Friedrich Delitzsch (1850–1922),[26] or the Old Testament texts will only apply to Jewish theology in the form of the Hebrew Bible which, however, is neither materially nor hermeneutically identical with the Old Testament.[27] Despite the need to value the literary and religio-historical value of the Old Testament texts and to be conscious of Jewish theology, which draws on the scriptures of ancient Israel, as a possible and authentic way of reading the texts, corresponding aberrations over the course of the history of the Church and the history of interpretation show that eschewing Christian and Christ-oriented interpretation is not only theologically inappropriate but also regularly led to a devaluation of the Old Testament and, by extension, often to a devaluation or even persecution of Judaism as well. Conversely, a Christian and Christ-oriented interpretation of the Old Testament is not in itself immune to taking on an anti-Jewish tendency, particularly if it sets up a sharp antithesis between Jesus Christ, understood as the definitive revelation of God, and the divine revelations to Abraham and Moses, regarded as provisional and obsolete.[28]

---

25. Cf. Fohrer, "Das Alte Testament," 291–94; Reventlow, *Hauptprobleme der alttestamentlichen Theologie*, 1–30.

26. Cf. Friedrich Delitzsch, *Die Grosse Täuschung*; on Delitzsch, see Lehmann, *Friedrich Delitzsch*, and on the aforementioned problem, see Hartenstein, "Wettergott," 79.

27. See Janowski, *Theologie und Exegese*.

28. See Emanuel Hirsch, *Das Alte Testament*, 30; Bultmann, "Weissagung," 252–55.

In the context of Christian biblical *theology*, the Old Testament must be understood from the perspective of the New Testament (and vice versa), yet without flattening the literary and religio-historical uniqueness of the Old Testament (or of the New Testament) and without vilifying Judaism. Here, the subject of "Jesus Christ" takes on a key role, since it is the decisive link between the two Testaments. Otto Procksch formulated this in programmatic fashion:

> Through the figure of Christ, the Old Testament is brought into an indissoluble relationship with the New Testament. Yet beyond the causal relationship between the history of Israel and the history of the Church, there is also an analogy in their mutual spiritual structure. For just as the history of the Church has an eschatological focus in the return of Jesus Christ, the history of Israel has an eschatological focus in the historical appearance of Jesus Christ.[29]

As an alternative to the aforementioned ancient and medieval hermeneutics of the Church and to the modern attempts at a christocentric or christotelic interpretation,[30] there can be a biblical hermeneutics which traces the potential transferability of the understanding of God, the world, and humanity of the theologies found in the Old Testament, just as is the case in the New Testament traditions about Jesus Christ, and which points to structural correspondences, conceptual and thematic parallels, as well as traditio-historical connections in the discourse on God in the Old and New Testaments.[31] Such a *Christotransparent approach* aims to elucidate the Old Testament theologies that appear before, behind, and in the New Testament's discourse on Jesus as Christ, Lord, and God:

> Jesus Christ is not mentioned in the Old Testament, but the reverberations of his nature and the way in which God enacts his unfailing covenant of grace also finds an echo therein [. . .].[32]

---

29. "Durch die Gestalt Christi ist demnach das Alte Testament mit dem Neuen in unlösliche Verbindung gebracht. Es besteht nun aber neben dem Verhältnis der Kausalität zwischen der Geschichte Israels und der Kirchengeschichte das der Analogie auch in dem beiderseitigen geistigen Aufbau. Denn wie die Geschichte der Kirche einen eschatologischen Brennpunkt in der Wiederkunft Jesu Christi hat, so die Geschichte Israels in der geschichtlichen Erscheinung Jesu Christi." (Procksch, *Theologie*, 11).

30. Enns, *Ecclesiastes*, 27–29.

31. Cf. Preuß, *Das Alte Testament*, 120–40.

32. "Jesus Christus wird im Alten Testament nie erwähnt; aber der Widerhall seines Wesens und der Art, wie Gott seinen nie versiegenden Bund der Gnade in Kraft setzt, findet auch auf seinen Seiten ein Echo [. . .]." (Klaiber, *Biblische Grundlagen*, 81).

Here, especially regarding the background of the concept of the messiah, it is necessary to cross the boundaries of the canon and to take into consideration the Jewish writings from the Hellenistic and Roman periods that did not ultimately become part of the canon. Inasmuch as the subject of "Jesus Christ" grew out of the Old Testament, a historically-oriented presentation, such as Martin Kähler (1835–1912) has already convincingly shown, can only occur in hindsight,[33] without always being able to refer explicitly to the respective points of contact in the New Testament. That is, within the context of thematizing Jesus Christ as the subject of theology, even a historical-critical reading of the Old Testament should not avoid interpreting Old Testament texts with a view to Jesus Christ or interpreting Jesus Christ from the perspective of Old Testament texts; rather, it should make such interpretations methodologically transparent.[34] Finally, in contrast to older approaches that understood themselves as radically historical-critical,[35] the post-biblical history of reception should (once again) be taken more thoroughly into account, and the potential of "pre-critical" Jewish and Christian exegesis from Late Antiquity and the Middle Ages should be discovered anew.[36] Within the present context, the latter is only possible in certain cases.

3. Jesus Christ as Reflected in the Names of God in the Old Testament

3.1. Theology as Onomastics

As was already shown in the chapter on *El Shaddai*, theology can be understood as an argumentative development of the meanings contained in the name of a god or goddess, the horizons of meaning opened by this name, its historical background, as well as its narrative and functional contexts. The beginnings of a theology understood in this way can be found in reflection on the name of the Israelite-Jewish deity Yahweh, the so-called tetragrammaton (Exod 3:14); the Israelite-Jewish divine title *Shaddai* in Isa 13:6 (par. Joel 1:15); or on the name of the Greek god Zeus by Plato (*Crat.* 396a). With a view to biblical theology, such an approach is especially pertinent for two reasons: first, the name Yahweh can be regarded as

---

33. Kähler, *Jesus und das Alte Testament*, 5–12; cf. Dohmen, "Hermeneutik, II. AT," 1649–51; Brueggemann, *Theology*, 732.

34. Cf. Barton, "Messiah," 365–79; Waschke, *Der Gesalbte*, 157–69.

35. See the pointed remark in Fohrer, "Das Alte Testament," 294.

36. On this see, for example, Schwienhorst-Schönberger, "Das Hohelied," as well as the program of the series *Herders Theologischer Kommentar zum Alten Testament* founded by Erich Zenger (cf. Zenger, "Was sind Essentials," 234–38).

the veritable center of the Old Testament,[37] which is reflected in the New Testament at the beginning of the Lord's Prayer ("hallowed be thy name," Matt 6:9). Second, the double name formed by the personal name "Jesus" (ישוע as the short form of יהושע, יהושע / Ἰησοῦς) and the title "Christ" (משיח, משיחא / μέσσιας, χριστός) programmatically encapsulates the New Testament. Thus, when read as a sentence, the name Jesus Christ means "(The one who is called) 'Yahweh is deliverance' (is) the Anointed One/ Messiah."[38] On the basis of the divine names used in the Bible, the Old and New Testaments can be read as a reflection of the history of Yahweh and Jesus Christ. A textual linchpin of such an approach oriented around the names "Yahweh" and "Jesus Christ" is the motif of the transferral of God's name to Jesus Christ in Phil 2:9–11 (cf. Isa 42:8).[39]

3.2. *Yahweh—Kyrios—the Lord*

In the Old Testament, the divine name Yahweh is by far the most commonly used, the most religio-historically and theologically significant, and the most powerful with respect to understanding and speaking of Jesus Christ. Within the Old Testament, it occurs around 6,700 times. The oldest datable attestations are found in inscriptions from the ninth/eighth century BCE and theophoric personal names in the oldest kernels of the traditions about Samuel, Saul, and David from the tenth/ninth century BCE, which contain the element *yāh/yǝhô/yô* (cf. *'ǎdoniyyāh/Adonijah*, *yǝhônātān/Jonathan*, or *yô'āb/Joab*). The etymology and original pronunciation of the name יהוה are uncertain. The biblical tradition connects the name with the Hebrew verb היה ("to be/become") and interprets it as "the constantly existing one" (Exod 3:13–15). Greek transcriptions of יהוה as Ιαουε, Ιαουαι, Ιαβε, or Ιαβει among specific Church Fathers from the third to the fifth centuries CE as well as Semitic philological considerations suggest the pronunciation "Yahweh." Just as debated as the etymology of the name are the religio-historical origins of Yahweh.[40] According to the presumably oldest texts in Israelite cultic poetry,[41] Yahweh was originally a weather god, similar to the god Baal/*Hadad* who was venerated in northern Syria during the second and first millennia BCE. Whether Yahweh

---

37. Zimmerli, *Grundriß*, 11.

38. See §4.6 below (pp. 90ff.) and Vischer, *Das Christuszeugnis* (6th ed.; 1943), 7; Hofius, "Ist Jesus der Messias?" 106.

39. On the recent discussion of the transfer of the title κύριος, see Zimmermann, *Die Namen des Vaters*, 195–96; Vollenweider, "Der Name," 180–84.

40. Van Oorschot and Witte, *The Origins of Yahwism*.

41. Cf. esp. Ps 29* and Ps 93*; for a detailed discussion, see Müller, "The Origins of YHWH."

always had his home in Palestine or was brought there by a group of Yahweh-worshipers that immigrated to Palestine—the so-called "Moses cohort"—cannot be determined on the basis of the source material presently available. One piece of evidence, however, suggests that the worship of Yahweh as a weather god has its origins in Palestine.[42] The phenomena of fire, thunder, and earthquake described in the context of Yahweh's appearance at Sinai (cf. Exod 19:16, 18) are typical elements of a theophany report and are not dependent on a particular geographical setting. The Old Testament's references to Yahweh's appearance at Sinai,[43] like the inscriptions from Kuntillet ʿAjrud—contrary to a widely held scholarly view—hardly constitute evidence for Yahweh's original location in northern Arabia or in the region of Edom. Rather, they only indicate that Yahweh (also) revealed himself there and was (also) venerated there during a certain period of time.[44]

The preferred use of the personal name Yahweh in the Old Testament indicates the Old Testament's personal understanding of God. The literary point of departure for a theological evaluation of Yahweh's nature is Yahweh's self-presentation found in Exod 3:14, which also appears in Hellenistic Judaism and in the New Testament.[45] Two main features of the Old Testament's understanding of God emerge from this self-presentation: Yahweh eludes a particular definition and is above all human control. He is a God who acts, not one who rests in his own self-sufficiency; his significance does not consist of his (mere) existence but instead in his (acting) presence. The Old Testament does not convey a static but rather a dynamic understanding of God that is strongly connected to life and vitality.

Beginning around 300 BCE, the tetragrammaton was read as *ʾădonāy* ("Lord"; literally "my lords") and around 200 BCE was also replaced literarily by the epithet אדני. Concurrently, beginning around the middle of the third century BCE, the Greek translations of the Hebrew (and Aramaic) scriptures of Israel translated the tetragrammaton with κύριος ("Lord"). Through these processes, the aspect of the universal rule of the Israelite-Jewish God also came to the fore at a linguistic level. Thus, through the use of the title "Lord," Yahweh's character as an Israelite-Jewish national deity was systematically universalized and correlated with other classical and ancient Near Eastern conceptions of divinity, in which a number of gods bear the title "Lord" (*baʿal, bel, mārāʾ*).[46]

---

42. Cf. Pfeiffer, "The Origin of Yhwh."
43. Cf. Exod 19:1–Num 10:10; Deut 34, Deut 33:2, Judg 5:4–5, Ps 68:9.
44. For a detailed discussion, see Pfeiffer, "The Origin of Yhwh."
45. Cf. Philo, *Det.* 160; *Mut.* 11; *Somn.* 2.230–31, and Heb 11:6, Rev 1:4, respectively.
46. Martin Rösel, *Adonaj*, 36–55, 228.

Like the human use of the term "Lord" to indicate a differential of power, the use of the term "Lord" with reference to Yahweh places the worshiper and his or her environment in a particular relationship to God. A key theological function of this divine title is the relativizing of all other forms of power, whether claimed and exercised by other people or applied to rulers who were venerated as gods in other religions. According to the understanding of the Old Testament, the title "Lord" ultimately does not belong to any king, but to God alone.[47] Addressing Yahweh as Lord is on the one hand a profession of his unique and absolute authority encompassing every area of life, and on the other hand an expression of the limitless trust in his power. By addressing Yahweh as Lord and by rendering the tetragrammaton with κύριος, it was possible to identify Yahweh with Jesus Christ, who is addressed as κύριος already in the New Testament (cf. Rom 10:9, 1 Cor 8:6). In this respect, Ps 110:1 probably played an important mediating role (cf. Mark 12:34–36).[48] A significant factor in this identification, which began in the New Testament and was subsequently developed in the early Church and allowed the Lord Jesus Christ to be seen as acting in the role of the Old Testament *Kyrios*, was the fact that the New Testament authors primarily used the scriptures of early Judaism in their *Greek* version, first using them as their Bible in the form of the Septuagint, which later became the Old Testament. In this way, Jesus Christ not only became a successor of Yahweh but also took on the role of universal ruler provided by the epithets אדני/אדון and κύριος.

3.3. King—Shepherd—Sebaoth and Almighty

Like the other deities of the ancient Near East and of classical antiquity, in the Old Testament Yahweh can be addressed by a number of titles and given a variety of epithets. The Psalms, which are directed at Yahweh as prayers of entreaty, thanksgiving, praise, and lament, are particularly rich in this area. Here, every epithet has its own religio-historical background, its own specific sociocultural and literary usage, as well as its own function with reference to God, who is thereby attributed a particular role. Individual epithets can overlap with others in terms of their motifs and can vary in the images they invoke and in their function. A number of the most important epithets for Yahweh reappear in the New Testament,[49] whether with reference to the God of Israel, from which aspects of the particular correlation between Yahweh and Jesus can be derived, or as a form of

---

47. Exod 15:11, Jdt 9:7–9, Esth 4:17a LXX.
48. Feldmeier and Spieckermann, *Der Gott der Lebendigen*, 43.
49. Zimmermann, *Die Namen des Vaters*.

addressing Jesus himself, whereby Jesus appears as a successor of Yahweh (as in the case of the title Kyrios) and from which a particular Christological understanding can be derived.

3.3.1. *Yahweh as King*

The reference to Yahweh as king has its religio-historical origins in Syrian-Canaanite polytheism.[50] It presupposes a pantheon ruled by the god who is designated as king. Such a hierarchical pantheon is attested in ancient Near Eastern religion beginning in the third millennium BCE. In the worship of Yahweh, the designation of Yahweh as king appears throughout the first millennium BCE and reflects a transferral of elements from the worship of Baal as well as an adoption of solar motifs ("solarization").[51] Thus, the well-known formula "Yahweh is king" in Pss 29, 47, 93–99 is based in the myth of Baal's succession to the throne following his defeat of the god of the sea Yammu, as is attested at the northern Syrian coastal city of Ugarit (Ras Shamra).[52] Related to the designation of Yahweh as king are the description of God's rule over the celestial "sons of God" (בני אלים, בני האלהים),[53] the description of the heavenly throne,[54] the conception of Yahweh's kingly actions in heaven and on earth,[55] as well as the conception of the future kingship of God that is attested in the eschatological texts of the Old Testament and in the non-canonical early Jewish apocalypses.[56]

From a theological perspective, the designation of Yahweh as king fulfills a dual function. On the one hand, the use of the title of king allowed originally non-Yahwistic conceptions of divinity to be incorporated into the worship of Yahweh. In this respect, Yahweh appears less as king over Israel than as king over the Egyptian, Assyrian, Babylonian, Phoenician, or Syrian gods, who were incorporated into his heavenly entourage and were thus subordinated to him.[57] On the other hand, as in the case of the title "Lord," all human rule is relativized through the designation of Yahweh as

---

50. Cf. Ps 98:6, Isa 6:5, Jer 46:18; on this, see Smith, *The Origins of Biblical Monotheism*, 41–80.

51. Janowski, "JHWH und der Sonnengott," 192–219; Keel, *Die Geschichte Jerusalems*, 380–85, 416–20; Leuenberger, "Die Solarisierung des Wettergottes," 34–71.

52. Cf. the Baal Cycle *CTA 2/KTU* 1.2 (trans. Dennis Pardee [*COS* 1.86.245–249]; Manfried Dietrich and Oswald Loretz [*TUAT* 3:1118–34]; Herbert Niehr [*TUAT.NF* 8: 195–202]).

53. Frequently translated as οἱ ἄγγελοι in LXX (cf. Job 1:6, 2:1, 38:7; Ps 82:1, 6; 97:9).

54. Isa 6:1, Ps 47:3–9, 93:1–2.

55. Ps 103:19.

56. See §4.6 below (pp. 90ff.).

57. Cf. Pss 29, 47, 96, 135.

king (cf. Pss 82, 146). The latter is highlighted in the superlative title for Yahweh, "King of Kings," which was used especially in Jewish texts from the Hellenistic period and was continued in the New Testament's reception of the title.[58]

3.3.2. Yahweh as Shepherd

From a religio-historical point of view, the reference to Yahweh as a shepherd is closely related to that of Yahweh as king.[59] Referring to a god as a shepherd was common in a number of classical and ancient Near Eastern religions and brings together the aspect of powerful rule on the one hand and the benevolent and responsible exercise of power on the other. As such, the shepherd metaphor is found with reference both to the deity and to the king. The Old Testament's references to Yahweh as a shepherd are based on this ancient Near Eastern conception. In this way Yahweh can be described as the shepherd of the individual supplicant (Ps 23:1) as well as of the entire people of Israel (Gen 49:24, Ps 80:2). In combination with the rendering of the tetragrammaton by κύριος, the reference to Yahweh as a shepherd constitutes an important literary and thematic background for the New Testament's descriptions and interpretations of the life of Jesus.[60] Within the context of typological interpretation,[61] this concept also found iconographic expression, such as when in Ps 23:1 the "Lord" is identified with Jesus Christ, who is depicted as a shepherd.[62]

3.3.3. Yahweh as Sebaoth and as the Almighty

Sebaoth (צבאות) is a genuinely Hebrew epithet for Yahweh, while the title "Almighty" was first introduced into the history of the religion of Yahweh by the Septuagint, which translated the Hebrew terms צבאות and אל שדי with the term παντοκράτωρ ("All-ruler"). This term, in turn, was translated in the Latin Bible as *omnipotens* and by Martin Luther as "Almighty" ("Allmächtiger").[63] The title *Sebaoth* has particularly military connotations, as it stands for "Yahweh, the God of the armies." It describes Yahweh as the warrior deity who goes out to battle before the army (צבא)

---

58. Cf. Sir 51:12n (H^B), Deut 9:26 LXX, Esth 14:12 LXX, and 1 Tim 6:15, Rev 17:14, respectively.
59. For a detailed discussion, see Janowski, "Der gute Hirte," 247–71.
60. Cf. Mark 14:27 (as a quotation from Zech 13:7), John 10:11, Heb 13:20.
61. See §2.2 above (p. 56).
62. Cf. Stuttgarter Psalter, Cod. bibl. fol 23 [60] – 28v, on Ps 23 [22]. In this description, the messianic etiology has been influenced by the "Protevangelium" in Gen 3:15: http://digital.wlb-stuttgart.de/purl/bsz307047059/page/60 (02/16/2017).
63. Witte, "El Shaddai," p. 26 in the present volume.

of Israel (1 Sam 17:45), as the leader of the celestial armies (i.e., the stars: Isa 45:12, Neh 9:6), as the lord of the heavenly court (i.e., the angels),[64] or as the head of all earthly and heavenly beings.[65] The Septuagint rendered the divine title "Yahweh Sebaoth" very often as κύριος παντοκράτωρ ("the Lord Almighty," especially in the Book of the Twelve) and thereby laid a cornerstone for the identification with Jesus Christ, such as was made explicitly by Martin Luther (1529) in the song "A Mighty Fortress is Our God," which drew on Ps 46, or implicitly by Georg Weisel (1623/1642) in the adaptation of Ps 24 in the song "Raise High the Door." As was shown above, the designation παντοκράτωρ, which was used especially in Hellenistic Judaism, reflects the all-encompassing authority of God, which is articulated in his role as creator, judge, and military protector.[66] In early Christianity, the title παντοκράτωρ with reference to Jesus Christ marked Christ's universal rule and position against pagan gods who bore this title,[67] while the title *Sebaoth* remained restricted to God the Father in distinction to the Son.

3.4. Yahweh as Father

In contrast to the Old Testament epithets mentioned above, which were applied to Jesus Christ in the New Testament or in the early Church, the reference to God as father (אב / πατήρ), which was used as a form of address to God by Jesus himself (cf. Mark 14:36, Matt 6:9) and which plays a central role in the later development of the conception of Jesus as the Son of God (cf. Matt 11:27), remains limited to Yahweh alone. The Old Testament only refers explicitly to Yahweh as father in a limited number of instances and reserves such a characterization for the metaphorical description of the relationship between Israel and its God or between God and the king. The reference to Yahweh as the father of the individual believer is not attested in the Hebrew texts of the Old Testament but is found in the Greek version of Ben Sira from the second century BCE and in a Hebrew text from Qumran.[68] In light of personal names that contain the element -ʾāb-, however, it is clear that Yahweh was also venerated in ancient Israel as "father," that is, as the personal protector of an individual.[69] Beginning

---

64. Isa 45:12, Ps 89:7–9, 103:21, 1QHᵃ XI, 22.

65. Gen 2:1, cf. Neh 9:6 with a focus on the heavenly army.

66. Cf. Witte, "El Shaddai," pp. 21–25 in the present volume.

67. See above, pp. 26–27 (with fig. 3) and n. 97.

68. Cf. Sir 23:1, 4 and 4Q372 1, 16, respectively; see also v. 10 in the Hebrew prayer that was added later to the book of Ben Sira in Sir 51:1–12 (Hᴮ).

69. Cf. Joab "Yahweh is [my] father" (1 Sam 26:6); Abijah "My father is Yahweh" (2 Chr 13:20–21).

in the exilic period (sixth century BCE), Yahweh is also described as father in the context of literary imagery and similes.[70]

In contrast to its use in other ancient Near Eastern religions, the infrequent use of the title "father" for Yahweh in the Old Testament serves to avoid resonances with Canaanite-Phoenician fertility cults. Thus, in the Old Testament, Israel, kings, and individual believers trace their relationship to God back to a personal and historical choice (בחר / ἐκλέγομαι) on the part of God and to a recognition (ידע / γινώσκω) and profession (ידה / ἐξομολογέω) of God on the part of humans. According to the Old Testament, the father-son relationship between Yahweh and the Judahite king is based in a historically conditioned choice or adoption, not in a mythical ancestry.[71] Functionally, it characterizes the temporal designation of the king as the representative of God as well as the earthly guarantor of divine order and justice (Ps 2:7, 89:27).[72] The functionality of the father-son metaphor is also reflected in its sapiential use with reference to a wise person who, by showing mercy to the poor, receives the title "son of God/son of the Most High" (Sir 4:10). The earliest profession that Jesus is the Son of God is in line with such a functional understanding (Mark 1:9–11). As a son, Jesus represents divine justice, the kingdom of heaven, and divine Wisdom.

Likewise, in the father-son relationship between Yahweh and Israel, the significance of the relationship is a dominant aspect.[73] At the center of the characterization of Yahweh as father is the idea of Yahweh's loving devotion to his people and Yahweh's demand for his people's obedience.[74] These two aspects, among others, can also be seen in the many references to God as the father of Jesus Christ and as the father of believers in the New Testament.[75]

The worship of Yahweh represented by the Old Testament—in contrast to the other religions of the ancient Near East but also in contrast to the archaeological and epigraphic evidence for the worship of Yahweh himself[76]—does not acknowledge a mother deity or a goddess of fertility,

---

70. Isa 45:10, 63:16, Mal 1:6, Ps 103:13, Prov 3:12.

71. Cf. 1 Sam 16:8–12 and Ps 2:7, respectively, and on this, Feldmeier and Spieckermann, *Der Gott der Lebendigen*, 49, 66.

72. See §4.6.1 below (pp. 92ff.).

73. Exod 4:22, Deut 1:31, Hos 11:1, Isa 1:2.

74. Deut 32:6, Isa 64:7, Jer 31:9.

75. Cf. 2 Thess 2:16, Matt 21:31; and on this, Zimmermann, *Die Namen des Vaters*, 41–166, esp. 164–65.

76. Cf. the inscriptions referring to "Yahweh and his Asherah" from Kuntillet ʿAjrud (ninth/eighth century BCE: Renz and Röllig, *Handbuch der Althebräischen Epigraphik*, vol. 1, 57–64; Davies, *Ancient Hebrew Inscriptions*, vol. 1, nos. 8.015–8.017; 8.021) and the

love, or war who was venerated alongside Yahweh. Nevertheless, certain female literary images and metaphors are used to describe the relationship between Yahweh and his people. Thus, Yahweh occasionally appears in the image of a child-bearing woman (Isa 42:14) or as a comforting, loving, and nurturing mother.[77] The metaphors in Exod 19:4 and Deut 32:11–12 draw on the image of the protective wings of a mother eagle.[78] Combined with epithets relating to divine wisdom (חכמה / σοφία), these feminine descriptions of God, which are to be understood relationally and functionally rather than ontologically, reappear in the New Testament in the application of the self-presentation of "Lady Wisdom" (Sir 24:19–23) to Jesus Christ (cf. Matt 11:28–30).[79]

3.5. "I Am" Statements

A succinct summary of the Old Testament's understanding of God is found in the self-presentation formula אני יהוה/ἐγὼ κύριος "I am Yahweh/I am the Lord" (cf. Exod 6:2, 6–7), which occurs more than two hundred times in the Old Testament. In this formula, which in its basic grammatical structure can disclose the revelatory speech or appearance of a deity just as in other ancient Near Eastern and Classical religions, the divine titles and epithets discussed above flow together in the received form of the Old Testament. Sometimes extended by phrases such as "the God of Abraham" (Gen 28:13, cf. Matt 22:32), "the one who brought you out (of Egypt)" (Exod 6:6–7), "your creator" (Isa 43:1), "your savior and your redeemer" (Isa 49:26), or "the first and the last" (Isa 48:12; cf. Rev 1:17), these "I am"-statements concretize the Old Testament's personal and relationship-oriented understanding of God, which is expanded Christologically in Jesus' "I am he"-statements[80] and especially in the revelatory speeches in the Gospel of John.[81] In Jesus' statement ἐγώ εἰμι, the late-Deuteronomistic phrase אני הוא (Deut 32:39) is taken up and sharpened: In Jesus Christ, Yahweh's very nature can be seen.

---

reference to Anat-Yahu in the Elephantine Papyri (fifth century BCE: APFC 44:3); on this, see van der Toorn, "Anat-Yahu," 80–101).

77. Isa 42:14, 49:15, 66:13; Hos 11:1–4, see also Num 11:12.

78. Or: mother vulture.

79. Cf. Luke 13:34, John 16:20–33; on this, see also Schimanowski, *Weisheit und Messias*, 313–14; Oeming, "Salomo-Christologie," 72–73.

80. Mark 13:6, Matt 14:27, cf. Isa 41:4.

81. Cf. John 6:48, 10:7, 14:6.

4. Jesus Christ as Reflected in the Experience of God in the Old Testament

4.1. The Old Testament as a Theological Interpretation of Experience

On the one hand, the Old Testament represents a collection of texts from a variety of religio-historical backgrounds, literary genres, and socio-cultural uses that developed over the course of several centuries. The Old Testament texts grew out of a process of continual selection, interpretation, and adaptation to new historical situations and thus reflect a number of different theologies. Within this process of supplementation and interpretation, a wide variety of cultic, legal, historiographic, and sapiential traditions are reflected. On the other hand, the individual blocks of tradition in the canonical forms of the Old Testament (the Hebrew Bible, Septuagint, and Vulgate) can be read as a reflex of fundamental experiences of existence interpreted as encounters with God. Inasmuch as the *Torah* and the *Nevi'im* (Joshua to Malachi) had largely reached the form in which they are known today by 300 BCE and 200 BCE, respectively, and were handed down as sacred scripture in early Judaism (alongside additional texts that did not become canonical), the "master narrative" spanning from the creation of the world to the hope in the establishment of the universal rule of the God worshiped at the cosmic mountain, Zion, and recognized as the lord of history already lay before the New Testament authors.

Thus, in what follows, the understanding of God that characterizes the individual blocks of tradition in the Old Testament will be discussed in terms of its religious and literary nature as a continual process of rereading as well as in terms of the continuation of this process with clear reference to Jesus Christ. This discussion of central statements about God in the Old Testament aims to clarify the understanding of God that characterizes the New Testament's discourse on Jesus as Christ, Lord, and God. Thus, topics such as "king and messiah,"[82] "messianic figures,"[83] or the "history of the concept and expectation of the messiah"[84] will intentionally *not* form the point of departure or the focus of the discussion, even though the Israelite-Jewish conceptions of kingship, the title "messiah," and messianic prophecies will naturally be mentioned with regard to their literary and

---

82. Cf. Day, *King and Messiah*.
83. Cf. Yarbro Collins and Collins, *King and Messiah as Son of God*.
84. Cf. Laato, *A Star is Rising*; Oegema, *The Anointed and his People*; Fabry and Scholtissek, *Der Messias*.

religio-historical backgrounds as well as their theological significance.[85] Rather, the point of departure for this presentation is the so-called final form of the books of the Old Testament. At the same time, reference to the literary history and tradition history of the texts is still necessary in order to understand the Old Testament's diverse discourses on and images of God and God's actions toward the world and humanity in their historical depth.

4.2. God as Creator: Jesus Christ as Reflected in Old Testament Theologies of Creation

The biblical canon and, by extension, the Christian creed, begin with the acknowledgment of God as the creator and thus as the one who gives meaning and guarantees existence to the world and humanity. Here the opening report of creation in Gen 1:1–2:3 does not stem from the oldest form of the religion of Yahweh but instead goes back to Priestly writers in the sixth/fifth century BCE. Drawing on Egyptian and Babylonian sources, these writers created a report characterized by the motif of the word (דבר / λόγος) of God and structured according to a seven-day scheme leading to the Sabbath, which served as a prologue to the foundation myth of Israel that culminated in the establishment of the cult at Sinai.[86] At the center of this report, which results in providing security to a world threatened by chaos and in a vow by God, who provides order and makes life possible, is the characterization of humanity as a representative of God in the world and as responsible to God for shaping the world. Taking up the ancient Near Eastern ideology of kingship in modified form, the Priestly authors of Gen 1 depict humanity as the "image of God" (*imago dei*; Gen 1:26–27). According to the Priestly understanding (also shared by the author of Ps 8), this description, which simultaneously depicts humanity in royal terms, applies to every human being, irrespective of gender, age, ethnicity, or religion. In the conception of the Priestly Writing, this gift and responsibility bestowed upon humanity at creation must be realized (Gen 6:13) and preserved (Gen 5:1–2, 9:4–6) even after and despite human failure.

Through its combination with the narrative of Adam and Eve and their sons Cain and Abel in Gen 2:5–4:26—which stems from an originally independent primeval history and was probably also composed in the sixth/fifth century in sapiential circles and was later revised at points in light of Gen 1:1–2:3, where it now functions as an interpretation of the latter—

---

85. See §4.6.1 below (pp. 92ff.).
86. Exod 25–40*; cf. Gen 2:3 with Exod 40:33.

the Priestly view of humanity and thus also the relationship between God and humanity was complicated significantly. The conception of the sovereign creator-God in Gen 1 is set in contrast with the image of God as a punishing judge in Gen 3. The kingly human in Gen 1 is countered by the debased human who hides before God in Gen 3. The vitality of humanity emphasized by the blessing of multiplication in Gen 1 is contrasted with the prospect of mortality and the hope in eternal life in Gen 3. The human who was called and equipped to shape the world in Gen 1 is juxtaposed with the human who, despite having knowledge of what promotes life and what destroys it,[87] kills his brother and is thereby confronted directly by death in Gen 3–4. Despite all of the failures that humanity experiences in the events constructed as a paradigm for human existence, what remains constant is the relationship to God as the one who gives life, who is known as the creator, and who can be invoked in prayer (Gen 4:25–26). In this respect, prayer represents a fundamental human constant.

The essential elements of the primeval history in the Old Testament— behind which stand the general, timeless experiences of ordered and chaotic structures in nature, the inaccessibility of life, the ambivalence of human existence, as well as the hope in a meaningful life and in overcoming the limitations of death—call for a narrative and thematic continuation. With a view to the Bible as a whole, the concepts of the creative word of God that continues to be active in history, of a regular return to the most intensive communion with God in any place made possible by the inauguration of the Sabbath (Exod 20:8–11, 31:13–17), and of the tension between humanity's being created in God's image but suffering under its creaturely limits, all of which are expressed in the primeval history and developed further in other Old Testament traditions, find their apex in their focus on Jesus Christ. Mediated by Hellenistic Jewish speculation on the role of Wisdom and *logos* in creation,[88] Jesus Christ takes on three distinct roles. First, Jesus Christ can be identified as the single creative word of God[89] or as the decisive mediator of creation.[90] Second, Jesus Christ can be explained as the one who enables direct contact with God and thus as a personification of the Sabbath, which also explains Jesus' freedom with respect to Sabbath observance.[91] Third—and this point is of particular

---

87. This is how the Hebrew expressions for "good" (טוב) and "evil" (רע) in Gen 2:9, 17; 3:5, 22 may be paraphrased.

88. Prov 8:22–31, Sir 24, Wis 7:21–30, 9:9, *1 Enoch* 42; Philo, *Ebr.* 31; *QG* 4.97; *Conf.* 146.

89. John 1, Rev 19:13.

90. Col 1:15–17.

91. Mark 2:23–3:6.

significance for the development of Christology—following ancient Near
Eastern and Jewish conceptions of the ideal, wise *Urmensch*[92] and Jewish
reflection on the relationship between the first Adam (Gen 1:26) and the
second Adam (Gen 2–3),[93] Jesus Christ can be understood as a new Adam
(Rom 5:12–21; 1 Cor 15:21–22), as a true human being (*ecce homo*; John
19:5), as a true image of God (Col 1:15), and as the provider of eternal
life (1 Cor 15:23).

4.3. *God as Companion: Jesus Christ as Reflected in the Theologies of the Ancestral Narratives*

An essential theological feature of the ancestral narratives in Gen
11:27–50:26, which were composed of different Priestly and non-Priestly
sources between the eighth and the fourth centuries BCE, is the conception of God as a companion (cf. Gen 46:2–4). As such, God places himself
in a relationship with humanity through his blessing, his promises of land,
progeny, and community, as well as through the establishment of a "covenant"—more precisely, a "commitment" (ברית / διαθήκη)—to humanity,
preserving people even in life-threatening situations, provided that they
trust firmly in God. In their final compositional form, the ancestral narratives offer a combination of a theology of obedience to God, who has
committed himself to humanity (reflecting Priestly tradition; cf. Gen 17),
a theology of trust in God, even when he shows his dark side (reflecting an
"Elohistic" tradition; cf. Gen 22), and a theology of blessing, which God,
in his freedom, accords to those who are paradigmatically chosen by him
(reflecting a "Yahwistic" tradition, cf. Gen 12:1–3). In addition to these
aspects are elements from Israelite-Jewish sources that were integrated at
a very late stage in the redaction of the ancestral narratives, such as the
strange story of the war of Abraham and his 318 servants against the kings
of the east in Gen 14, whose theological message can be encapsulated in
the notion that God can do powerful things through those who are weak
(cf. 2 Cor 12:9) and which was interpreted allegorically in the early Christian *Epistle of Barnabas* as reflecting the salvation brought about by Jesus'
death on the cross, as well as various late redactional passages, such as Gen
15 or Gen 18:20–33, which are of particular theological significance when
considered with a view to the Bible as a whole.

The narrative of Yahweh's self-revelation in Gen 15,[94] which is influenced by both Deuteronomistic and prophetic language and which takes

---

92. Job 15:7, Sir 17:7, 4Q504 8r 4–7.
93. Cf. Philo, *Opif.* 69; *Leg.* 1.31–42.
94. Gen 15:1: "I am your shield," cf. Ps 3:4, 33:20.

the form of a prophetic oracle of salvation[95] in its promise of a son and of land to Abraham,[96] indicating Abraham's faith (i.e., his unconditional trust) as an indicator of unconditional faithfulness to communion with God,[97] takes on a particular significance in the overarching context of the Pentateuch, the prophetic books, and the New Testament. On the one hand, through his faith/trust (אמן [*Hiphil*] / πιστεύω), Abraham is placed alongside figures such as Moses and Samuel.[98] On the other hand, Gen 15:6 is reinterpreted in Hab 2:4 to mean that the righteous person will survive the eschatological cosmic judgment through his or her unconditional trust or faithfulness.[99] To that effect, Paul interprets Gen 15:6 to mean that God grants humans justice (δικαιοσύνη)—that is, communion with God, which is accessed through faith in God's saving actions through Jesus Christ (Rom 1:16–17). The foreshadowing in Gen 15:13–21 of Israel's sojourn in Egypt and subsequent exodus reaches its climax in the identification of Yahweh as the judge of all of those who oppress Israel (Gen 15:14) and constitutes a prelude in Israel's early history to Yahweh's universal eschatological judgment.[100]

The dialogue between Abraham and Yahweh in Gen 18:20–33, which goes back to a late reworking concerned with the theology of justice, connects thematically to the flood narrative in Gen 6–9 in its question of whether God wipes out the just and the unjust in equal measure and how many righteous people there must be in a city in order to rescue such a city from being destroyed by divine retribution.[101] Like the flood narrative, this dialogue thematizes the problem of divine justice. The notion that ten righteous people could ultimately rescue Sodom from destruction (Gen 18:32) is one of the forerunners of the conception of the substitutional, expiatory death of the sole Righteous One who would give his life for many by undergoing divine judgment.[102] The paradigmatic nature and openness to reinterpretation of the dialogue between Abraham and Yahweh can also be seen in the fact that Abraham identifies himself as "dust and ashes"—in other words, as a human *par excellence*—in a profession of lowliness that has its place in the late piety of the Psalms (Gen 18:27; cf. Ps 103:14) as well as in the fact that Gen 18:24, 28 only speak of "the city" in

---

95. Cf. Isa 41:10–16.
96. Gen 15:7, cf. Gen 17:8, 18:10.
97. Gen 15:6, cf. Neh 9:8, Sir 44:20.
98. See Num 12:5 and 1 Sam 2:35, 3:20, respectively.
99. See pp. 46–48.
100. Cf. 1 Sam 2:10, Isa 3:13, Ps 7:9, Acts 17:31, Rev 18:4–5.
101. On this, cf. Levin, *Der Jahwist*, 168–70.
102. Cf. Isa 52:13–53:12, 1 Pet 2:22–25, and on this, Janowski and Stuhlmacher, *Der leidende Gottesknecht.*

generalized terms. In this way, Gen 18:23–33 is a reflection of the destruction of Jerusalem in 587 BCE, a plea for every city to have ten just people in its midst, and a prelude to Jesus' weeping over Jerusalem (cf. Luke 19:41). Through the literary dialogue in Gen 18:23–33—which, like Gen 15, features the profession that God is the judge of the world[103]—Abraham appears as an exemplary intercessor[104] and as the model for the dialogical dispute with God, which has unconditional faith as its basis. This theology has a counterpart in the figure of Job, who is often compared with Abraham in post-biblical tradition,[105] and it is transformed in the image of Jesus praying in Gethsemane (Mark 14:32–36).[106]

At the center of the discourse on Yahweh in the ancestral narratives is the experience of Yahweh's intervention in the lives of individual people. Yahweh takes on human behaviors insofar as he blesses and promises, makes commitments, and accompanies people. Yahweh speaks to people but is also silent; he reveals himself but also hides himself; he appears in familiar places but also in places where no one expects him, allowing such places to be designated as the house of God (בֵּית־אֵל, Gen 28:16). In the ancestral narratives, God has both light and dark sides: the God who chooses and blesses Abraham is the same one who tests (or "tries") Abraham and demands that he sacrifice his only and beloved son.[107] The God who regards Abraham's faith as a sign of his trust in God is the same one who wrestles with Jacob in the night and leaves him wounded.[108] The God who gives fertility to Leah and Rachel is the same one who allows Abraham to send away Hagar, the mother of his son Ishmael, without rights or protection.[109] What is common to these different aspects of the discourse on God is the fact that God takes part in the lives of individuals. According to the ancestral narratives, God is not a disconnected, ahistorical, and faceless being but rather has a personality.

Here, two themes above all permeate the theology of the ancestral narratives: the theme of blessing and the theme of the journey. Thus, Gen 11:27–50:26 narrates how God promises a blessing, how this blessing is constantly in danger, and how it is enacted. These elements of the promise of blessing, the threat to that blessing, and the enactment of the blessing

---

103. Gen 18:25, cf. Ps 96:13, Acts 17:31, Rev 19:11.
104. Cf. Job 42:8, as well as the ironic references in Isa 63:16, John 8:39.
105. Here, the parallel between Gen 18:27 and Job 30:19, 42:6 is particularly in view; on this, see Witte, "Hiob und die Väter Israels," 39–61.
106. Cf. Luke 22:39–46, John 17.
107. Cf. Gen 12:1–3 with Gen 22:1–2.
108. Cf. Gen 15:6 with Gen 32:26.
109. Cf. Gen 29–30 with Gen 16 par. 21.

always take place on a journey made by the individual figures in the ancestral narratives. In this way, within the context of the Pentateuch, the ancestral narratives prefigure the narrative of the exodus from Egypt and the entry into the land under the leadership of Yahweh and his servant Moses (Exodus–Joshua*), which was originally composed as an independent founding myth.[110] Moreover, within the context of the Bible as a whole, the ancestral narratives prefigure the narrative shaping of Jesus' life as the story of a journey. For the latter, the concept of the participation in the blessing of Abraham, which is exemplified in the motif of being children of Abraham (Isa 51:2, 63:16), plays a central role when Jesus Christ is placed within the genealogy of Abraham (Matt 1:1); when the rite of circumcision (Gen 17), which was inaugurated with Abraham, is sharply contrasted with the freedom from the law made possible through Jesus Christ;[111] or when the notion of being children of Abraham is fundamentally called into question (Matt 3:7–9; cf. John 8:56).

4.4. God as the Unique Liberator, Leader, and Teacher of Israel: Jesus Christ as Reflected in the Theologies of the Exodus and Sinai Traditions

The narrative complex that spans the books of Exodus through Deuteronomy, which was created through the separation of the exodus narrative from the narrative of the entry into the land in the book of Joshua as well as through the gradual integration of late Priestly material (Leviticus; Numbers) and of Deuteronomy,[112] has three focal points, each with a specific conception of God. Thus, the exodus narrative per se (Exod 1–15) has the main theological theme of Yahweh's liberation of Israel. In the wilderness narratives (Exod 16–18; Num 10:11–36:13), the theological theme of Yahweh's accompanying or leading of Israel—despite Israel's antagonism against God—predominates. Embedded within the narrative of the wilderness wandering is the report of Israel's encampment at Sinai and the giving of social and cultic laws (Exod 19:1–Num 10:10), which has the main theological theme of Yahweh, who reveals himself to his people as the only God who is to be worshiped and who as a teacher instructs his people in all of the fundamental areas of social and religious life. The speech of Moses in Deut 1–33, which takes the form of a will or

---

110. Cf. Kratz, *Die Komposition der erzählenden Bücher*, 314–27; Gertz, *T&T Clark Handbook of the Old Testament*, 263–66.

111. Cf. Gen 17 with Gal 4 and Rom 4.

112. Cf. Kratz, *Die Komposition der erzählenden Bücher*, 324–30; Gertz, *T&T Clark Handbook of the Old Testament*, 266.

testament and marks the end of the Mosaic period, repeats and interprets events from the exodus, wilderness, and Sinai traditions, provides a new set of laws, and alludes to Israel's future. In this speech, the theological high points of the exodus, wilderness, and Sinai narratives reach their culmination: Yahweh is the unique liberator, leader, and teacher, who gave his chosen people the "law of life" (Sir 17:11 LXX, 45:5)[113] in the form of the Torah.

4.4.1. The Exodus-Eisodus Narrative

Within the exodus-eisodus narrative, Yahweh's act of leading the Israelites out of Egypt represents the foundational event in Israel's history. Alongside Yahweh's self-revelation at Sinai, the exodus is Israel's most basic profession of Yahweh's salvific acts. Here, theology is soteriology. As in the ancestral narratives, several different literary strata can be identified in the depiction of the exodus, all of which have distinct theological features: a multi-layered non-Priestly source (divided into a "Yahwist" and an "Elohist" in earlier scholarship), a Priestly source, a Deuteronomistic source, a later redactional layer combining Priestly and Deuteronomistic elements, as well as numerous other literary expansions that cannot be situated precisely.

The theological differences within the exodus-eisodus narrative are exemplified in the different literary depictions of Moses. At the center of the Priestly depictions of Moses is the notion of Moses as a mediator between God and humanity. Moses is the representative of Yahweh and the founder of the cult, yet is himself not without flaws (Num 20:1–12, 22–29). According to the Priestly worldview, his cultic mediation is necessary, since there is no direct relationship between God and humanity. The Deuteronomistic layer emphasizes Moses' role as a representative. Thus, the (late-)Deuteronomistic Moses takes upon himself the guilt of his people—namely, their constant disobedience of Yahweh's demand to be worshiped alone (Exod 32:32, Num 11:11–17)—and is described as an unrivaled prophet (Deut 18:15, 34:10). In the non-Priestly and non-Deuteronomistic texts, Moses can appear, on the one hand, as a charismatic leader (cf. Exod 3:11, Num 11:24–25). His role focuses on emphasizing the inaccessibility and transcendence of God, but these do not abrogate the personal relationship between God and humanity. On the other hand, Moses can be described in these texts as a messenger and interpreter (cf. Exod 7:16–17) as well as an intercessor (cf. Exod 8:26).

113. Cf. Witte, "'Das Gesetz des Lebens,'" 109–21.

In the received form of the Pentateuch, all of these aspects of the figure of Moses are combined into the multifaceted image of a literary biography. The "miniatures" of Moses in a number of late Psalms[114] and in Jewish writings from the Hellenistic period[115] add further aspects to the glorification of Moses. In addition to Moses' stylization as the writer of the Torah to the extent that Moses' name can become synonymous with the Torah itself,[116] Moses' glorification culminates in the description of him as a "divine man" (θεῖος ἀνήρ) and in the conception of a Moses that returns or is resurrected at the end of time (*Moses redivivus*).[117] These notions form the background to the numerous Moses-typologies and Moses-antitheses developed by the New Testament authors in their descriptions and interpretations of the person and life of Jesus Christ and which culminate in the motif of Jesus Christ as the new Moses.[118]

Connected to the different images of Moses is the motif of the miracles performed by God in the plagues of Egypt, the deliverance of Israel at the Sea of Reeds, and the preservation of Israel in the wilderness, which is characteristic of the theology of the exodus-eisodus narrative and is also significant in Jesus' demonstrations of power as narrated in the New Testament. In the Priestly layer of the plagues narrative, the plagues are "proofs" or "legitimation miracles" for Yahweh's demands received by Moses and presented to the pharaoh by Aaron. They serve to demonstrate Yahweh's power in Egypt and cause the pharaoh to appear as Yahweh's puppet, drawn through his stubbornness into Yahweh's plan for history.[119] In contrast, in the non-Priestly layer, the plagues are divine "coercive miracles" that serve to break the pharaoh's resistance and to demonstrate Yahweh's justice in punishing the recalcitrant pharaoh.[120] Similarly, the Priestly Writing stylizes the deliverance of the Israelites at the Sea of Reeds as a miracle and a demonstration of the greatness of Yahweh, who uses Moses to part the sea and to allow the Israelites to pass through.[121] From

---

114. Cf. Ps 77:21, 103:7, 105:26, 106:16, 23, 32; see also Ps 90:1.

115. Cf. Sir 45:1–5, Wis 10:15–11:1; Artapanus, *Fr. 3* (*OTP* 2:898–903); Philo, *Mos.*

116. Cf. Mark 12:19, Luke 16:29, 31, 24:27.

117. Cf. John 1:21, 6:14, 7:40 against the background of Deut 18:15, 18; Bousset and Gressmann, *Religion*, 233; Jeremias, "Μωυσῆς," 860–61, 871–78.

118. Cf. esp. Matt 5–7, Mark 10:1–12, Acts 3:22, 7:37; and on this, Saito, *Die Mosevorstellungen.*

119. Cf. Exod 7:13, 22, 8:15, 9:12.

120. Cf. Exod 7:23, 8:11, 28, and on this, Schmitt, "Tradition der Prophetenbücher," 44–58.

121. Cf. Exod 14:1–4, 21, 27, and on this, Schmitt, "'Priesterliches' und 'prophetisches' Geschichtsverständnis," 209–13.

a religio-historical perspective, this Priestly depiction of the divided sea[122] reflects a critique of the Babylonian creation myth, according to which the god Marduk disposed of the primeval sea creature Tiamat,[123] and reflects a hermeneutical pattern for interpreting a historical event through recourse to myth that is fundamental to the theology of the Old Testament. In the New Testament's reflections on Jesus Christ, this pattern appears when the historically-experienced salvific action of God in Jesus Christ is given narrative shape in the motif of Jesus' mythic power over the sea[124] and the miracle is understood as a reference to divine intervention that is made accessible through faith. In the non-Priestly portions of the narrative of the miracle at the sea, the emphasis is instead on the unique salvific action of Yahweh.[125] Yahweh alone fights as a warrior for his people[126] by bringing an easterly wind to push back the water of the sea[127] and by causing a divine fear to take hold of the Egyptians. The key words "history" and "liberation" sum up the theology of the exodus narrative in its received form. In the exodus, Yahweh is experienced in a unique historical event. The recognition of Yahweh's nature as God appears in the form of a report about his historical actions. Similarly, the recognition of God in the New Testament also has a narrative structure inasmuch as the history of Jesus Christ is narrated as the history of God's actions.

The wilderness narratives—which form a literary frame around the Sinai pericope, are redactional elaborations on the themes of the "exodus," "Sinai," and "entry into the land" and go back to local traditions of different groups or are conscious literary constructions—revolve around existential threats to Israel in the "wilderness" (thirst, hunger, enemies). A fundamental aim of these narratives is to present the wilderness generation as a prototypical Israel and to present Moses the intercessor as a model of the Priestly intercessor in the case of the confession of guilt. The "wilderness" describes the exilic reality that began with the fall of Israel in 722/720 BCE and of Judah in 587 BCE; it serves as a cipher for the exile and for the Jewish Diaspora; and it is an object lesson of human and divine history. Thus, from a theological perspective, the wilderness is a significant place for experiencing both divine presence and divine absence

---

122. Cf. Josh 4:21–23, Neh 9:9–11, Ps 74:13–15, 106:7–10, 22; Isa 51:10–11, 63:12–13.
123. Cf. the Babylonian creation epic *Enūma Elish, Tablet IV,* trans. Benjamin R. Foster (*COS* 1.111:396–99); Karl Hecker (*TUAT. NF* 8:106–12).
124. Mark 4:35–41, 6:45–52.
125. Cf. esp. Exod 14:13–14, 15:21b.
126. Cf. Exod 15:3, Isa 40:10, 42:13.
127. Cf. Deut 11:4, Josh 24:6–7, Ps 66:6, 114:3–5, Nah 1:4.

(cf. Mark 1:12–13). The central image of God in the wilderness narratives is the conception of Yahweh as a saving warrior, a sustaining creator, and an accompanying protector.

Irrespective of the question of how the exodus-eisodus events and the revelation at Sinai relate to each other historically, the literary combination of both of these elements of tradition produces the theological concept of Yahweh's salvific action ("salvation-indicative"), from which Yahweh's concrete commandments follow ("salvation-imperative"). The liberation granted by Yahweh is the prologue to the instructions given by Yahweh. The exodus, which reveals Yahweh as a liberator and leader, is followed by the revelation of Yahweh as the sole lawgiver and teacher.

4.4.2. The Sinai Pericope

The greater part of the Sinai pericope consists of the divine commandments communicated to Moses[128] and the law (νόμος, *lex*) in the narrower sense, which will be "repeated" in Deuteronomy. Perhaps the oldest core of the tradition—which is also the most important passage in the Sinai pericope for the New Testament's interpretation of the death of Jesus—is the theophany narrative in Exod 24. This theophany concludes in the communion (through a shared meal) between a self-revealing God and those who receive the revelation (Exod 24:1–2, 9–11). This theophany was secondarily connected to a sacrifice (Exod 24:4b–5) and to a blood ritual (Exod 24:6, 8a), and communion with God was reinterpreted in terms of the concept of "covenant," which stems from ancient Near Eastern treaties and is already familiar to the reader coming from Gen 15 and Gen 17.[129] Here, the relationship between God and God's people is illustrated by an altar, which symbolizes Yahweh's presence. The blood sprinkled by Moses as the medium of the life force serves as a binding power between God and God's people. Deuteronomistic and Priestly circles played a significant role in developing the theological concept of the "covenant." In these circles, the "covenant" was interpreted on the one hand as an obligation of Israel resulting from the divine promise (cf. Deut 28:69) and on the other hand as a solemn commitment on the part of God himself (cf. Gen 17:2). At a tertiary stage of development, extensive legal materials were integrated (in multiple stages) into the Sinai pericope as a counterpart to the "covenant," the observance of which, according to the Deuteronomistic and post-Deuteronomistic understanding, sustains life (Deut 30:15–20). Wherever Israel's fate in exile was understood as resulting from a breach in

---

128. Exod 25–31, 34; Leviticus; Num 1–10 et al.
129. Exod 24:8, cf. 1 Cor 11:25, Heb 9:20.

the "covenant," and wherever the reason for such a breach was traced back to human nature as insufficient, tending toward evil (or "life-destroying"), and therefore sinful, such as in late texts within the book of Jeremiah,[130] it is almost inevitable that the hope in a new "covenant" created by God and a radical transformation of humanity through God will also appear.[131]

In the received form of Exod 19:1–Num 10:10, two theological concepts come to the fore: first, the Deuteronomistic theology of Israel's obedience to the first commandment, and second, the Priestly theology of the expiatory cult.[132] Both theologies are linked through the notion that Yahweh is the only God and as such should be worshiped without the use of images (Exod 20:4; cf. Deut 5:8). At the same time, however, the demand for exclusive worship and the prohibition of images constitute the basic characteristics of Old Testament monotheism shared by both Jesus himself and all of the New Testament authors.[133] This received a decisive modification in the identification of Jesus Christ as God, which is found already in the New Testament (John 20:28), and in the mediation of the relationship between God and humanity through Jesus Christ in the Trinitarian dogma.

Nineteenth-century Old Testament scholarship already recognized that the Yahweh-monotheism reflected in the Old Testament is the result of a long religio-historical development. Within this process, Yahweh, who was originally worshiped locally alongside other gods and goddesses, gained ascendancy as the one and only God through various political, economic, and cultural factors and by incorporating other deities' features and areas of activity. The historical origins of the worship of Yahweh alone (*monolatry*) as the deity of a group of people named "Israel" in central Palestine, yet which did not exclude the existence of other gods (cf. Exod 22:19), could go back as far as the pre-monarchic period (twelfth/eleventh century BCE) and could have been related to the understanding of Yahweh as the guarantor of justice (cf. Exod 22:21–26). A decisive part of this development, however, occurred after the establishment of the kingdoms of Israel and Judah with the concentration of the state and temple cult of both of these kingdoms on Yahweh beginning in the ninth/eighth century BCE. During this process, the worship of other deities alongside Yahweh (particularly the goddess Asherah) initially remained untouched in the so-called family religion of Israel and Judah. For example, outside of Judah,

---

130. Jer 13:22, 17:9, cf. Gen 6:5, 8:21, Job 25:4–6, 1QHª XII, 29–31.

131. Jer 31:31–34, Ps 51:7–10, cf. Heb 8:8–10, Luke 22:20, 1 Cor 11:25, 2 Cor 3:6; on this, see Schmitt, *Arbeitsbuch zum Alten Testament*, 200–204.

132. See §4.5 below (pp. 86ff.).

133. Cf. Matt 6:24, Rom 3:29–30, 1 Cor 15:28.

the worship of a certain Anat-Yahu alongside Yahu (Yahweh) continued on the island of Elephantine (Jeb) in southern Egypt into the fifth century BCE. In contrast, in the state religion of Israel and Judah, the worship of other gods and goddesses was suppressed beginning in the eighth century BCE, accompanied by the application of solar concepts to Yahweh under Neo-Assyrian influence.[134] Following the fall of the kingdom of Israel in 722 BCE, this process was given further theoretical underpinning by Deuteronomistic theologians in Judah during the seventh/sixth century BCE. The role that monarchic-era Israelite and Judahite prophecy (eighth to sixth centuries BCE) played in this development—against the view of earlier scholarship, which saw in such prophecy the theological origins of Yahweh-monolatry and Yahweh-monotheism—is difficult to determine. Since the prophetic books of the Old Testament continued to be reworked into the third century BCE, passages that can be understood as monolatrous or even monotheistic[135] could possibly be the result of a correspondingly late process of supplementation.

The decisive impulse for the development of Yahweh-monotheism was the fall of the kingdom of Judah in the sixth century BCE and, with it, the end of the official state cult. In the context of the Babylonian exile (587–520/515 BCE) and the Jewish Diaspora, the conception arose of a worship of Yahweh that was no longer tied to the temple in Jerusalem but that could instead be practiced anywhere. Significant catalysts for such a development included the encounter of the Jewish elite with the Babylonian worship of Marduk, which experienced a shift toward the worship of Marduk alone,[136] as well as with Persian Zoroastrianism, which focused on the god Ahura Mazda.[137] Based on their comparison of Yahweh with the other deities of the ancient Near East, Jewish theologians in the sixth/ fifth century BCE arrived at the notion of Yahweh's incomparability (Isa 40:17–18). Historical events were now interpreted as the actions of the sole God who acts in history, Yahweh.[138] With respect to the experience of chaos that was manifested in the destruction of the Jerusalem temple, the stylization of Yahweh as the sole creator of heaven, earth, humanity, and nature[139] served a paracletic and apologetic function—namely, to

---

134. See §3.3.1 above (pp. 66ff.) and Janowski, "JHWH und der Sonnengott," 192–219.

135. Cf., for example, Hos 2:19, 4:12, 8:4–6, 9:10, 10:1–6, 11:2, 13:1–2, and on this, Vielhauer, *Das Werden des Buches Hosea*.

136. On this see Albani, *Gott*, 75–122.

137. Hutter, *Religionen in der Umwelt*, 200–201, 237–41; Koch, "Die Religion der Iraner," 88–115.

138. See §4.6 below (pp. 90ff.).

139. Gen 1:1–2:4; Pss 8, 104; Job 38–39; Isa 40:12; 45:18.

strengthen trust in Yahweh's faithfulness and to depict Yahweh as superior to all of the other creator deities of the ancient Near East. At the end of the Babylonian exile, a restoration of the Davidic kingdom with the earthly king as Yahweh's representative did not occur (Ps 2:7, 110:1), but instead the theologically developed concept of the uniqueness of the heavenly king Yahweh came to the fore.[140] As creator, driver of history, and God of Israel, Yahweh is necessarily the one and only God (Mal 1:11). Even with the re-building of the Jerusalem temple, which became the center of the religion of Yahweh during the Persian and Hellenistic periods, this idea did not disappear. The *Shema Israel* (Deut 6:4–5), which possibly dates back to the seventh century BCE and originally emphasized the unity of Yahweh over the worship of Yahweh in different manifestations and in different places ("poly-Yahwism"),[141] was now understood as declaring the uniqueness of Yahweh, who correspondingly took on the title of "the One" (אחד / εἷς).[142] With this title, Yahweh was later pitted against the Hellenistic supreme deities, whether Zeus, Sarapis, or Isis, who could also be invoked as "[the] one god."[143] The confrontation of Jewish sages and scribes with Hellenistic rulers' claims to universal rule and with the supreme deities propagated by them gave significant momentum to Yahweh-monotheism. At the end of the literary and conceptual development of the concept of Yahweh's uniqueness in the Old Testament is the expectation that one day the entire world will recognize and worship the one and only God Yahweh.[144]

Characteristic for pluralistic Yahweh-monotheism during the Second Temple period (520/515 BCE–70 CE) is the development of angelology and demonology. Thus, during the Persian and Hellenistic periods, Yah-weh was conceived of as a king enthroned in heaven and surrounded by heavenly beings,[145] whereby Yahweh's majesty, transcendence, and good-ness (in contrast to a growing number of evil angels and demons[146]) could be emphasized.[147] In this way, monotheism was preserved but took on mildly dualistic traits.[148]

---

140. Isa 43:10–11, 44:6, Deut 4:35, 39, 32:39.

141. On this, cf. Exod 20:24, 2 Sam 15:7 and the inscriptions from Kuntillet ʿAjrud (Renz and Röllig, *Handbuch der Althebräischen Epigraphik,* vol. 1, 57–64; Davies, *Ancient Hebrew Inscriptions,* vol. 1, no. 8.015–8.017; 8.021).

142. Cf. Job 23:13, 31:15; Zech 14:9; on this, see Witte, "Der Glaube an den einen Gott," 245–62.

143. Markschies, "Heis Theos," 209–34.

144. Isa 2:2–3, Zech 14:16.

145. Cf. Job 33:23, Tob 3:16, 12:12, 15; 4Q400–407.

146. Cf. *1 Enoch* 6–9, *Jub.* 5:1–20.

147. Cf. Tob 3:16, 12:15.

148. Cf. *Jub.* 17:15–18, which draws on and reinterprets Gen 22.

Within this milieu of diverse beliefs in the one and only God, who as such is also the only Good (הטוב / ὁ ἀγαθός)[149] but is nevertheless surrounded by a host of heavenly mediators and figures of different classes, the figure of Jesus himself arose,[150] and it is in this context that the person of Jesus was interpreted by the New Testament authors.[151]

Even if the historical origins of Yahweh-monotheism are unclear and the phenomenon is ultimately without analogy, according to the Old Testament the origin of the worship of Yahweh alone has to do with the very nature of this deity: Yahweh is the אל קנא (θεὸς ζηλωτής), a God who zealously pursues his goal.[152] In this way, Yahweh's zeal connects to the absoluteness of his relationship to his worshipers and to the unconditionality of his recognition. Through Yahweh's zeal, Yahweh's love and holiness are expressed. Yet inasmuch as love and holiness are characterized by exclusivity, uniqueness, and personality, monotheism goes hand in hand with Yahweh's very nature. The holy zeal of Yahweh can be seen especially in the (late-)Deuteronomistic stylization of certain prophetic figures, particularly Elijah (1 Kgs 18, 2 Kgs 1:2–17) and Jeremiah (Jer 11–20*), who speak up unconditionally for the worship of Yahweh and as such provided the model for the representation of Jesus as a prophet who is zealous for Yahweh's holiness.[153]

The emphasis on Yahweh's uniqueness is accompanied by the ambivalent evaluation of older practices associated with the worship of Yahweh and of contemporary non-Yahwistic cults. Monotheism is accompanied by a criticism of other gods and myths involving such gods. Thus, during the Persian and Hellenistic periods, the confrontation with other gods is reflected in the broadening of the prohibition against images, which originally only aimed at the making of cultic images in the context of the worship of Yahweh (Exod 20:4–5), to include a significant polemic against the cultic images of other gods.[154] Here, the prohibition against images appears as a counterpart to the command to worship Yahweh alone[155] and reflects the formation of religious boundaries and identity in Persian- and Hellenistic-period Judaism. The more the Torah became the focal point in early Judaism, the stronger the criticism of cultic images grew.

149. Cf. Nah 1:7, Ps 119:68, 145:9, Lam 3:25, Sir 45:25 (H^B), Mark 10:18, Luke 18:19.
150. Cf. Mark 1:13, Matt 13:41, John 5:4.
151. For a detailed discussion see Yarbro Collins and Collins, *King and Messiah as Son of God*.
152. Exod 20:5–6, 34:14, Num 25:11–13, Deut 4:24, 5:9, 6:15.
153. Mark 11:15–19 par. Luke 13:34; see §4.6.2 below (p. 97).
154. Cf. Isa 46:1; Jer 50:2, 38; 51:47, 52; and Dan 5; on this, see Ammann, *Götter*, 254–66.
155. Cf. Isa 40:18–20, 44:9–11, 46:5–8.

During this process, the Torah itself, as the authoritative instantiation of God's presence, took on the role of a cultic image (cf. 1 Macc 3:48). This scripture-oriented religiosity was accompanied by a harsh derision of the divine images of the surrounding religions,[156] which in the Hellenistic and Roman periods led to alienation from contemporary cults but also evoked a certain degree of admiration within pagan philosophical circles.[157]

The New Testament's description of Jesus Christ as the true image of God can be read as an intensification of the Old Testament's prohibition against images, in which the motifs of humanity's being created in the image of God[158] and of Wisdom as a reflection of divine glory (Wis 7:24–26, cf. Heb 1:3) are joined: while in Gen 1:26–27 humanity alone is a legitimate image of God, in Col 1:15–17 Jesus Christ alone is the true image of God.

4.5. *God as the Holy One: Jesus Christ as Reflected in Old Testament Conceptions of Holiness*

The majority of the commandments that were successively inserted into the Sinai pericope deal with cultic issues. The so-called cultic law[159] thematizes the separation between sacred and profane, between pure and impure, and thus connects to the conception of God as the Holy One par excellence. Inasmuch as humans find themselves separated from God on account of their createdness and sinfulness (Isa 6:5), the cult is the means by which and the place where humans can experience the beneficial presence of God and establish contact with God (cf. Ps 27:4). Generally, cultic practice involves a "holy time" (the regular performance of the ritual), a "holy place" (the bounded area of the sanctuary), "holy people" (the priesthood that is employed by the community to perform the cult), and "holy acts" (cultic rituals, which also involve "holy objects," such as an altar, and the recitation of "holy texts," such as myths or psalms). All of these elements are introduced in the narrative of Israel's experience at Sinai as a visible expression of the worship of Yahweh, the Holy One, by his "holy people Israel" (cf. Exod 19:6, Deut 7:6). Even though the cultic laws presented there appear in the mouth of Moses, they overwhelmingly reflect the rituals of the Second Temple (beginning in 520/515 BCE), and in part they reflect a literary fiction that is independent of the actual performance of the cult. Irrespective of whether individual rituals were

---

156. Cf. Baruch 6, Wisdom 13–15, DanBel.
157. Cf. Hengel, *Judentum und Hellenismus*, 475, 540, 555; Witte, "Worship and Holy Places," 289–303.
158. See §4.2 above (pp. 72ff.).
159. Exod 25–31, 34; Leviticus; Num 1–10, among many others.

actually performed or were only experienced virtually, the Old Testament's cultic regulations contain an extensive set of motifs and traditions that were interpreted in the New Testament with a view to Jesus Christ. The most significant of these include conceptions of the temple, priests, sacrifice, and expiation, while others include festivals and the different forms of prayer, particularly in the Psalter, inasmuch as (1) the latter represented the most important book of prayer and meditation in Judaism during the time of Jesus, (2) Jesus himself prayed particular psalms, and (3) the Psalter is the most frequently cited Old Testament book (and not only in the context of Christology).

A fundamental aspect of the Israelite-Jewish conception of the temple —from the time of the monarchies in Israel and Judah until the Hellenistic-Roman era—is the notion that the temple is the place where Yahweh is worshiped and is Yahweh's earthly abode (lit., "house," בית, היכל). As the "place of life,"[160] the salvific nearness of God and divine blessing can be experienced in the temple, which can also be expressed metaphorically as the shining of God's face[161] or as being in the light of God.[162] Over the course of the history of Israelite-Jewish literature and religion, four main theologies of the temple arose, each of which sought to resolve the tension between the conception of God as dwelling both in heaven and in the temple on earth. First, the temple can be understood as the place where, through God's invisible presence, heaven and earth meet (Isa 6:1)—the temple is accordingly Yahweh's footstool.[163] Second, Yahweh's dwelling place can only be located in heaven, while the temple represents the gateway to heaven (Gen 28:12, 17). Third, according to the Priestly Writing in particular and to Ezekiel's vision of the temple (Ezek 40–48), Yahweh can be imagined as present in the temple through his glory (כבוד / δόξα), which is understood as a transcendent form of light (Exod 40:34–35, Ezek 43:2). Fourth, there is the conception developed especially by Deuteronomistic theologians that Yahweh himself dwells in heaven but that his name (שם / ὄνομα) is present in the temple as an extension of his person (Deut 12:5).

During the Hellenistic period, while the Second Temple was still in existence,[164] these temple theologies underwent significant modifications, driven by factors such as the Diaspora situation, competition be-

---

160. Janowski, "Der Ort des Lebens," 369–97.

161. Num 6:24–26; Ps 95:6; 119:135; cf. 2 Cor 4:6; Hartenstein, *Das Angesicht JHWHs*, 194–96 passim.

162. Ps 27:1, 36:10, cf. John 8:12.

163. Ezek 43:7, Lam 2:1, Ps 99:5.

164. The history of the temple of Jerusalem after the destruction 587 BCE and before the rebuilding 520/515 BCE is uncertain. A small cult at the remains of the temple was possible (see Jer 41:5).

tween different Yahwistic sanctuaries in Jerusalem, Samaria, on the island
of Elephantine (Jeb) in Egypt,[165] and (beginning around 170 BCE) in the
Egyptian city of Leontopolis (*Tell el Yahudiya*), as well as by an individual-
istic impulse that is also attested in pagan thought and religion during this
period. The first such modification was a shift toward personal piety, which
is reflected in the so-called "post-cultic psalms";[166] the second was a shift
toward regarding the Torah as sacred, such that reading from the Torah
could replace the rituals performed at the temple;[167] and the third was the
formation of groups that understood themselves as the true congregation
of Yahweh and identified themselves as a temple.[168] Alongside the prohibition on images, the concentration on the Torah and on the true congregation of Yahweh that understood itself as a temple, the physical temple
receded into the background. This development finds radical expression
in the notion that Jesus Christ himself is the new temple (cf. Mark 14:58),
which was also influenced by the literary and eschatological motif of a new
temple (Ezek 40–48, Rev 21) and the historical experience of the destruction of the (second) temple of Yahweh in Jerusalem in 70 CE.[169]

The performance of the cult was the task of cultic personnel—that
is, the priesthood. During the monarchic period in Israel and Judah and
during the exilic period, a priestly hierarchy with decreasing levels of holiness developed. Until the exilic and post-exilic periods, the main task of
the priests was less the performance of sacrifice and instead the issuing of
oracles and instruction (תורה) on how to handle holy objects and how to
avoid impurity. The Deuteronomic program of cultic purity and unity in
Deut 12, which dates to the late monarchic period, was further developed
during the Persian and Hellenistic periods in the Priestly Writing and in
the "constitution" of Ezekiel in Ezek 40–48. According to these texts, the
pure cult of Yahweh consists of a strictly structured priesthood, with the
high priest, who is modeled in the figure of Aaron, at the top.[170] Those
under the high priest are priests who can trace their ancestry back to Aaron
and, like the high priest, must follow particularly strict purity regulations
and are not allowed to own land.

By the Second Temple period at the latest, the performance of sacrifice was one of the main tasks of the priests. The Old Testament does

---

165. On this, see Kratz, "The Second Temple," 247–64; ; Zangenberg, "The Sanctuary
on Mount Garizim," 399–418; Grancrød, *Dimensions of Yahwism*, 81–127.

166. Cf. Psalm 73; Stolz, *Psalmen im nachkultischen Raum.*

167. Cf. Pss 1, 19, 119; 1QHᵃ XIV, 10–18, XVI, 4Q400–407.

168. Cf. 1 Cor 3:16–17, 6:19; 2 Cor 6:16; 1QS VIII, 5, IX, 6, 1QSb III, 25–26, 4Q174
1 I, 21, 2, 6.

169. See Ego, Lange, and Pilhofer, *Gemeinde*; and Horn, "Ortsverschiebungen."

170. Cf. Lev 8:1–13, 21; Sir 45:6–22, 50:1–21.

not present a unified conception of sacrifice but instead speaks of different types of sacrifice, each with their own underlying meanings. For example, sacrifice could be understood as a gift to the deity, whereby the motivation for bringing the sacrifice allows one to differentiate between an offering of supplication or a thanksgiving offering. Alternatively, the sacrifice could be understood as a meal with the deity (*communio*) or as an offering of expiation. The intention behind all of these types of sacrifice was to influence the relationship between the sacrificer and the deity. In the Old Testament, approved sacrificial materials include plant and animal products as well as animals themselves but never humans, even though the offering of firstborn animals appears as a substitute for a family's firstborn child and the practice of human sacrifice in situations of extreme crisis is attested in ancient Israel's cultural environment (2 Kgs 3:27).[171] Thus, the notion of the death of a righteous person who "gives his life for many," which is found in the fourth servant song in the book of Isaiah (Isa 52:13–53:12) and is taken up in the New Testament as an interpretation of Jesus' death on the cross, represents an archaism but also a radicalization of the notion of the absolute holiness of God, whose will for communion with humans is so strongly affected by human sin that it requires the sacrifice of a sinless representative of humanity.[172] The New Testament's descriptions of Jesus as the sole true and sinless human (Heb 4:15, cf. *Pss. Sol.* 17:36) are based on this pattern of thought. Such depictions were complemented by the notion of expiation, which during the Second Temple period influenced not only the conception of sacrifice but also of festivals (cf. Sir 50:5–21), fasting (cf. *Pss. Sol.* 3:8), and almsgiving (cf. Prov 16:6, Sir 3:30, Tob 12:9).

Fundamental to the Old Testament's understanding of expiation is the notion that it is God who removes the guilt of humans and thereby allows for human expiation. To render expiation (כפר)[173] is thus primarily a salvific act by God.[174] This is enacted symbolically through a ritual performed on the Day of Atonement (יום הכפורים) and on other occasions whereby the sanctuary, the priests, and the cultic community are released from the sins of the past year when Aaron or the high priest transfers the sin to a goat, which is then sent into the wilderness ("scapegoat").[175] When the book of

---

171. On the question of human sacrifice and especially child sacrifice in the (early) worship of Yahweh see Bauks, "Theological Implications," 65–86; Lange, "They Burn Their Sons," 109–32; Pietsch, *Die Kultreform Josias*, 367–75.

172. Heb 7:26, 9:14, 1 Pet 2:21–24.

173. The LXX has a variety of equivalents: ἁγιάζω ("to sanctify"), ἐξιλάσκω/ἱλάσκομαι ("to forgive"), καθαρίζω ("to purify") et al.

174. Cf. Deut 21:8, 32:43, Jer 18:23, Ezek 16:63, 2 Chr 30:18, Ps 65:4, 78:38, 79:9.

175. Lev 16:8, 10, 20–22; on the "Day of Atonement," see also Lev 23:27–28 and 25:9.

Hebrews identifies Jesus Christ as the true high priest (Heb 2:17, 6:20), who only enters the holy of holies on the Day of Atonement in the cultic system of the Second Temple, and when Paul presents Jesus Christ as the "expiation" introduced by God (Rom 3:23–25, 5:11, cf. 1 John 2:2), the Old Testament and early Jewish conception of the God who grants expiation is elaborated upon (cf. Deut 21:8, 2 Chr 30:18–19, 1QH^a XII, 37).[176]

The Second Temple's Day of Atonement stands at the center of the autumnal festival of Sukkot, which originally celebrated the grape harvest, and the linguistic and visual associations of this festival are of paramount importance for the interpretation of the life and ministry of Jesus Christ. The same is true of the springtime festival of Passover and Maṣṣot, which was likewise originally connected to nature, marking the beginning of the barley harvest (cf. Lev 23:6–10, Deut 16:1) as well as the full moon, with a blood ritual aimed at dispelling demons, and was secondarily associated with Yahweh's historical action in the exodus (cf. Exod 12). Thus, in its Deuteronomistic and Priestly interpretation, the festival of Passover and Maṣṣot serves as a reminder of the liberation from Egypt. Each year during Passover-Maṣṣot, the experience of freedom is reenacted, which can also develop into a hope for an eschatological liberation in the form of a new exodus (cf. Isa 43:16–18). When the New Testament depicts the Last Supper as a Passover meal[177] or when Paul identifies Jesus Christ as the Passover lamb,[178] the Passion of Jesus becomes a new exodus. Just as God brought Israel out of Egypt, Jesus Christ also brings humanity out of the bondage of sin. Just as God freed Israel from slavery, God also freed Jesus Christ from death. In this way, the Old Testament's typology of the exodus,[179] which serves as a model for the future redemption of Israel,[180] is transformed christologically (Rev 15:1–3).[181]

4.6. *God as the Guide of History: Jesus Christ as Reflected in Old Testament Theologies of History*

In the foregoing discussions of God as creator; as the saving, promising, and protecting companion of Abraham, Isaac, Jacob, and Joseph; and as the liberator, leader, and teacher of the chosen people Israel, reference was already made to the theological motif of God as the master of history

---

176. Cf. 1QS XI, 14; 4Q512 29–32 9; CD-A II, 5, 18; IV, 9–10.
177. Cf. Mark 14:12–26, Matt 26:17–30, Luke 22:7–23.
178. Cf. 1 Cor 5:7.
179. See §2.2 above (pp. 56ff.).
180. Cf. Hos 2:17, 12:10, Mic 7:15, Isa 43:6.
181. Cf. Exod 15:1, Deut 32:4, Ps 111:2, 139:14, 145:17.

and, as the "everlasting God" (אל עולם / θεὸς αἰώνιος),[182] the master of space and time. This notion is developed in a variety of ways in the historical and prophetic books that follow the Torah. The historical crises of the fall of the kingdom of Israel to the Assyrians in 722/720 BCE and the conquest and destruction of Jerusalem by the Babylonians in 587 BCE, which were deeply impressed in Israel's cultural memory, stand in the background of the historical texts of the Old Testament, whether large-scale narrative compositions such as the history of the monarchy in the books of Samuel and Kings, which were redacted by Deuteronomistic authors (and later combined with the Deuteronomistic books of Joshua and Judges), or the large, primarily poetic prophetic books (Isaiah, Jeremiah, Ezekiel, and the Book of the Twelve, which was originally written on one scroll). In both cases, the dissolution of the political and cultic order of the state, whose official cult was that of the national deity Yahweh, led to a fundamental reflection among the spiritual elites of Israel and Judah over the power of Yahweh that resulted in the concept of Yahweh's universal authority over history, whereby Yahweh uses earthly powers as a means of instructing his people. It also led to the presentation of Israel's history as a linear process shaped by Yahweh according to the principles of guilt and punishment. In the received form of both the historical books and the prophetic books, this historical process has eschatological and occasionally even restrained messianic overtones.[183] In the prophetic books, it also has an apocalyptic element that no longer has in view a radical change in this world but rather a new world beyond the present one (Isa 24–27, Dan 7–12, *1 Enoch*). The Israelite-Jewish theologies of history in the Old Testament and the apocalyptic concepts that developed from these (as well as from certain sapiential traditions), which found expression in the early Jewish apocalypses that did not attain canonical status,[184] form an important conceptual background for the New Testament's interpretation of Jesus Christ as both a part of and the goal of God's actions in history, time and eternity.

Within the presentation of the history of the monarchy (1 Samuel–2 Kings), which was created primarily by Deuteronomistic redactors in the seventh/sixth century BCE through the reworking of older narrative cycles and court histories, as well as within the prophetic books, individual figures take on a special importance as paradigmatic vessels for implementing and interpreting Yahweh's plan for history. Rather than

---

182. Gen 21:33, Isa 40:28, cf. Sir 36:22 (H^B).
183. Cf. Beck, "Messiaserwartung"; Schmitt, "Der heidnische Mantiker"; Yarbro Collins and Collins, *King and Messiah as Son of God*, 25–47.
184. Cf. Collins, *The Apocalyptic Imagination*.

taking an approach that focuses on the historiographical and narrative structure of the historical and prophetic books, here the focus will be on these individual figures.

4.6.1. Yahweh's Kings

As elsewhere in the ancient Near East, kings in Iron Age Israel were conceived of as rulers installed by God, being regarded as earthly representatives of the divine order, high priests, and guarantors of justice and the welfare of the state (cf. Ps 72, Lam 4:20).[185] As in Mesopotamia and Egypt, in Israel and Judah the king could be described as a "son of God" (Ps 2:7, 110:1), albeit not in a biological but rather in an adoptive sense, and could be given divine attributes (Ps 45).[186]

A unique aspect of Israelite and Judahite kingship is the inauguration ritual of anointing the king, which probably reflects Hittite or West Semitic/Canaanite influence and served to symbolically endow the king with authority, power, and honor.[187] It is this ritual that led to the identification of the king as the "anointed one."[188] The anointing of the king as Yahweh's messiah expresses his special belonging to God, which is reflected in the bestowal of the divine spirit on the anointed one (1 Sam 16:13).[189] The functionality of the title *Messiah* can also be seen in the unique identification of a non-Israelite ruler, the Persian king Cyrus (Cyrus II, ca. 590/580–530 BCE) as messiah in Isa 45:1—significantly, in a text that post-dates the fall of the kingdom of Judah.[190]

In addition to the anointing of kings, the Old Testament also occasionally speaks of the anointing of prophets[191] (which is not a historically verifiable act but instead a theological qualification) and in postmonarchic texts also of priests, particularly the high priest,[192] who increasingly took on the role of the earlier Judahite kings during the Second Temple period. On one occasion, in a postmonarchic historical psalm, the ancestors appear as anointed ones (Ps 105:9–15 par. 1 Chr 16:16–22), which, like their designation as prophets (Gen 20:7), serves to express their particular belonging to Yahweh and reflects a late phenomenon of giving such figures honorary religious titles.

---

185. Cf. Witte, "Justice," pp. 38–42 in the present volume.
186. Cf. Yarbro Collins and Collins, *King and Messiah as Son of God*, 1–24.
187. Cf. 1 Sam 10:1, 16:1–13, 2 Sam 2:4, 1 Kgs 1:34, 2 Kgs 11:12, Ps 89:21.
188. 1 Sam 24:7, Ps 20:7, Lam 4:20.
189. On this see Feldmeier and Spieckermann, *Der Gott der Lebendigen*, 214–21.
190. Schmid, "Herrschererwartungen," 186, 195.
191. 1 Kgs 19:16 (Elisha as a successor of Elijah), Isa 61:1, cf. CD-A II, 12; VI, 1.
192. Exod 28:41, 29:1–3 and Lev 4:3, 6:15, Num 35:25, Dan 9:25–26, respectively.

The Israelite-Judahite royal ideology and its discourse on the king as the (current) messiah of Yahweh lies at the root of the so-called messianic expectations in the Old Testament and especially in early Jewish literature. Such expectations were directed at a future and final ideal king, a "son of David," who will fully enact Yahweh's rule on earth. From a religio-historical perspective, three factors led to the expectation of such a (royal) messiah in the strict or actual sense: first, the basic structure of ancient Near Eastern royal ideology, which always contains a future-oriented and utopian aspect ("present messianism")[193]; second, the real tension between ideal and reality within the kingdom from the ninth/eighth to the sixth centuries BCE; and third, the gradual romanticizing of the kingship of David (ca. 1000–960 BCE) as a "golden age." Under the influence of Nathan's oracle, in which David is promised an "everlasting dynasty" (2 Sam 7 par. 1 Chr 17), the (postmonarchic?) motif of the Davidic covenant,[194] the stylization of David as the exemplary chosen one of God (Ps 78:20), and the ultimate dissolution of Davidic kingship in 587 BCE, the hope in an imminent restoration first arose[195] and was followed by the notion of a future ideal Davidide or a *David redivivus*.

Significant Old Testament points of contact for this notion are prophetic royal oracles or promises ("messianic prophecies"). Their original historical context was the enthronement of kings. It was only in the context of the critique of the real king, found above all in the prophetic books, that they were applied to a future salvific king from the Davidic dynasty.[196] The beginnings of such a shift from royal oracles to an ideal figure in the near future probably occurred at the end of the eighth century BCE, but it only reached its full development in the kingless Second Temple period, when the oracles were developed into the concept of an ideal king in the distant future or at the end of time.[197]

These royal oracles and messianic prophecies, which (in light of their future-messianic understanding in early Christianity and in part also in Roman-period Judaism) included the eschatologically transformed royal psalms,[198] eschatological oracles relating to the tribes of Israel in the Pentateuch,[199] or the so-called Protevangelium,[200] contain multiple lit-

---

193. Waschke, *Der Gesalbte*, 167.
194. 2 Sam 23:5, Ps 89:4–5, 132:11–12.
195. Cf. Hag 2:23, Zech 4:6–7, with reference to Zerubbabel.
196. Isa 7:10–17, 9:1–6, 11:1–8, 16:4b–5, 32:1–8; Jer 23:5–6, 30:8–9, 33:15–16; Ezek 17:22–24, 34:23, 37:24; Hos 3:5, Mic 5:1–5, Zech 3:8, 4:1–14, 6:9–15, 9:9–10.
197. For the book of Isaiah, see, for example, Schmid, "Herrschererwartungen."
198. Pss 2, 20, 21, 45, 72, 89, 101, 110, 132, 144; see Saur, *Die Königspsalmen*.
199. Gen 49:8–12*, Num 24:15–24*.
200. Gen 3:15, cf. Rom 16:20, Heb 2:14.

erary layers. Most of these texts originated in the period after the end
of the Judahite monarchy. They reflect a process of repeated expansion
and updating and present different, historically conditioned conceptual-
izations of the expectation of a future salvific figure and are thus an expression of a particular eschatological, messianic concept.[201] They belong
alongside other eschatological concepts of salvation in the Old Testament,
particularly the expectation of Yahweh's future kingship,[202] and developed
out of negative experiences, either with the existing royal dynasty,[203] with
war and destruction,[204] or—in the late Hellenistic period—with dissatis-
faction over the status of the Jerusalemite priesthood. In the latter case, it
cannot be ruled out that some motifs were borrowed from the Hellenistic
ruler cult.[205]

Common elements of the Old Testament messianic prophecies—in
which the term "messiah" is never used and instead code names[206] or ci-
phers[207] are used, and whose designation as "messianic" is only due to
their explicitly messianic *relecture*[208]—include the proximity of the eschatological savior figure to Yahweh and his rule; the (spiritual) endowment
and commissioning by Yahweh; the bringing of peace, law, and justice for
all Israel; and the figure's connection to the Davidic dynasty. The latter
element is found especially in expectations that include a restoration of
the Davidic monarchy.[209] These texts do not reflect a unified picture of
the messiah; thus, a powerful and wise ruler figure[210] can stand alongside a
poor and humble king who is rescued by Yahweh.[211] The latter stylization
is influenced by the designation of the pious as poor and humble (before
God), a motif that is found especially in post-exilic psalms ("the ideal of
poverty/the piety of the poor").[212]

Alongside the conception of an individual eschatological savior figure and ruler, a collective messianic concept also arose in Old Testament
texts from the Persian and Hellenistic periods, likewise as a reaction to the

---

201. Oegema, *The Anointed and his People*, 290–306.
202. Fabry and Scholtissek, *Der Messias*, 12.
203. Isa 11:1–9, Mic 5:1–3, Jer 23:5–6.
204. Zech 9:1–10.
205. Ps 110 LXX, Zech 9:9–10 LXX; cf. Yarbro Collins and Collins, *King and Messiah
as Son of God*, 48–54.
206. Isa 7:14, Jer 23:6, Zech 6:12, Ps 132:17.
207. Isa 11:1, Jer 23:5, Ezek 17:22.
208. Waschke, *Der Gesalbte*, 13–16; Fabry and Scholtissek, *Der Messias*, 20.
209. Isa 16:4b–5, Ezek 37:24–25, Hos 3:5, Amos 9:11–12, Hag 2:10–23.
210. Isa 9:5–6, 11:5.
211. Zech 9:9 (according to the Hebrew text); cf. Hab 3:13, Ps 20:7.
212. Cf. Ps 22:27, 37:11, 69:33, but also Num 12:3.

fall of the actual monarchy.[213] Here, Israel or the ideal community (and possibly also Zion as their local personification) takes on the role of messiah (Isa 61:1–3).[214] In this collective version of messianic expectation, the declaration that Yahweh is the God of Israel and that Israel is the people of Yahweh takes on eschatological overtones (cf. Isa 32:15–18). The election of Israel as Yahweh's people, which is based in the exodus event and the revelation at Sinai (Exod 19:5–6, Deut 7:6–8) and was realized in the giving of the land and in statehood, finds its continuation in the eschatological role of Israel as the mediator of Yahweh's salvation to the nations (Zech 8:20–23; cf. John 4:21–26).

On the whole, messianic expectations do not play a central role literarily or theologically in the Old Testament. They are (only) one element in the traditio-historically and thematically diverse eschatologies in the Old Testament. Nevertheless, in the received form of the prophetic books, the eschatological ruler prophecies often appear prominently at the end of both smaller and larger textual units[215] as well as at key points in the Psalter.[216] Likewise, in the narrative arc of the Pentateuch, they appear in the transitions between major periods.[217]

Reinforced by the opposition of Jewish circles first to the Diadochoi, then to the Hasmoneans, Romans, and ultimately the Herodians, whereby the sacred scriptures of Israel were reworked and interpreted from an eschatological perspective,[218] the messianic promises in the Old Testament owe their special theological significance to two religio-historical and literary developments in Judaism during the Hellenistic and Roman periods.

First is the variety of expectations of eschatological savior figures within different eschatologically oriented Jewish groups between the second century BCE and the first century CE. Examples of such expectations are found in *Psalms of Solomon* 17 and 18, which know of the motif of a sinless messiah/Christ (*Pss. Sol.* 17:36), certain texts from Qumran such as 1QSa II, 11–21, where, based on the current state of knowledge, the absolute designation המשיח "the Messiah" for an eschatological savior figure is first attested,[219] as well as the first-century CE apocalypses in the

---

213. Isa 32:15–20, 55:1–5, Jer 33:16, Ps 89:51–52, 149:5–9.
214. See Schmid, "Herrschererwartungen," 187–89.
215. Cf. Isa 7*, 9*, 11*, 45*, 55*, 61*; see Schmid, "Herrschererwartungen," 179, 183–95.
216. Cf. Pss 2, 72, 89; see Christoph Rösel, *Die messianische Redaktion*.
217. Cf. Gen 49:8–12*, Num 24:15–24*.
218. See §2.3 above, pp. 57ff.
219. Cf. also 1QSb V, 20–23, 4Q174 1 I, 21, 2, 10–13, 4Q252 V, 3; as well as the so-called "Son of God text," 4Q246. On messianic conceptions at Qumran, see the literature cited on p. 96 (n. 227).

"parables" of the first book of Enoch (chs. 37–71)[220] and in the fourth book of Ezra (*4 Ezra* 7:28–29).

Second is the New Testament's reception and interpretation of Jesus of Nazareth as the anticipated Messiah, which drew on early Jewish messianic concepts.[221] Through the use of "Old Testament" messianic traditions and those in the contemporary milieu of early Judaism, Jesus became the Christ and the son of David born in Bethlehem.[222] Following the resurrection, this conception took on additional ruler motifs from both Israelite-Jewish and pagan Hellenistic traditions, such as being born of a virgin[223] or "sitting at the right hand of God."[224]

In addition to its main influence from Davidic royal ideology, the presentation of Jesus as the Messiah also incorporated Priestly and prophetic messianic ideas. Here, the aforementioned reference to the anointing of priests and prophets in the Old Testament stands in the background. The New Testament also shares these two configurations with certain strands of early Judaism. Thus, for example, the writings from Qumran also attest the notion of a priestly messiah[225] and a prophetic messiah.[226] As in the New Testament's identification of Jesus as the Messiah, in Qumran texts and other early Jewish texts, the boundaries between the notions of a royal, priestly, and prophetic messiah are fluid.[227] Here, both the early Jewish and the New Testament figurations of the messiah could take on traits of other figures from Israel's primeval and early history who were stylized as redeemers (Noah, Enoch, Moses, Elijah) or of the "son of man" (*1 Enoch* 48:2),[228] even if these figures did not bear the title "messiah."

What is theologically decisive for the Israelite and early Jewish theologies of history, in which God acts through a present, future, or eschatological king, is their thoroughly theocentric structure: God is the one who chooses the king unconditionally and independently. Even in texts where

---

220. Cf. esp. *1 Enoch* 48:10, 52:4.

221. Cf. Isa 7:14 in Matt 1:23; Mic 5:1, 3 in Matt 2:6; Zech 9:9 in Matt 21:5; Isa 61:1–2 in Luke 4:18–19.

222. Matt 1:1, 2:6, Mark 10:47; but see also the critical objection of Karrer, "Von David zu Christus," 346–47.

223. Cf. Matt 1:23, Isa 7:14 LXX.

224. Cf. Acts 7:55–56, Rom 8:34, 1 Pet 3:22, and Heb 1:13–14 with Ps 110:1.

225. 1QS IX, 11, CD-A XII, 23–XIII, 2, XIV,18–19, CD-B XIX,7–11: in each case, this is combined with a second *political messiah*; cf. *T. Sim.* 7, and as background Zech 4, 6:9–15, 1 Sam 2:35 LXX.

226. 4Q521 2 II, 1, 11Q13 II, 18; cf. also 4Q175 5–8 and 1 Macc 14:41 against the background of Deut 18:15, 18 and Isa 61:1; see §4.4.1 above (pp. 78ff.).

227. Zimmermann, *Messianische Texte aus Qumran*, 470–80; Evans, "Messiahs," 537–42; Fabry and Scholtissek, *Der Messias*, 36–52; Frey, "Die Textfunde von Qumran," 281–90.

228. See §2.3 above, pp. 57ff.

the eschatological messiah takes on divine traits, he remains a tool used by God and is subordinate to the kingship of God.

4.6.2. Yahweh's Prophets

Alongside kings, prophets stand out in the major theopolitical writings of the Old Testament as shapers and interpreters of divine history. In the Deuteronomistically redacted book of Kings and in the Chronistic history (Chronicles–Ezra–Nehemiah), which is dependent on the former, the prophets appear as fearless advocates of Yahweh who, at key turning points in history, stand up against the kings of Israel and Judah who fail to observe Yahweh's *Torah*. These prophets call for the worship of Yahweh alone and the observance of cultic and social laws and in some cases perform miracles (1 Kgs 17:11–24, 2 Kgs 5:1–14). In contrast, the literary biographies found in the prophetic books—which created the prophetic figures of Isaiah, Jeremiah, and Ezekiel through a process of literary expansion spanning several centuries—reflect figures who receive divine visions and oracles, pronouncing Yahweh's judgment and salvation to Israel, the nations and ultimately the entire world, emphasizing Yahweh's proclamations through symbolic actions[229] and interpreting historical processes from Yahweh's perspective.

In the places where the continually updated, reinterpreted, and reworked collections of prophetic oracles developed into portraits of prophetic figures, a defining element of being a prophet is the motif of the prophet's suffering, which is created by his contemporaries who oppose his prophetic mission. In the "confessions" of Jeremiah (Jer 11–20*), which were only added at a post-Jeremianic stage of composition,[230] and in the related "servant songs" in the Deutero-Isaianic layer of the book of Isaiah,[231] suffering becomes the marker par excellence of a prophet's life (cf. Jas 5:10–11). Through his suffering, the prophet chosen by God becomes a model of God who suffers on behalf of Israel and the world, and the prophet finds his ultimate justification and purpose in the act of substitution. Here, the connection made between the proclamation of God's justice and universal rule, which forms a common thread throughout the prophetic books, and the notion of the righteous sufferer, who embodies God's justice and rule,[232] is theologically significant and is central in the New Testament's reception of these concepts.

---

229. Cf. Isa 20:1–6, Jer 13:1–11, Ezek 4:1–6:14.
230. On this, see Bezzel, *Die Konfessionen Jeremias*.
231. Isa 42:1–4, 49:1–6, 50:4–9, 52:13–53:12.
232. See §4.6.3 below.

It is not possible to discuss here the complex religio-historical and literary development of the diverse theologies found in the prophetic books. With regard to the topic of Jesus Christ as the subject of Old Testament theology, it is significant that Jesus Christ, with his message about the βασιλεία τοῦ θεοῦ and his suffering, fits seamlessly within the line of Old Testament prophets as reflected by and in their books (cf. Luke 13:31–34, John 9:17). Here the motif of the righteous sufferer, particularly as found in the Passion narrative, reflects the influence of an early Jewish theology of martyrdom, which sees a substitutionary function in the death of the righteous sufferer (4 Macc 6:29, 17:22) and represents its own particular theology of history.

4.6.3. *Yahweh as the Lord of Time*

As the one who directs individual and collective destinies, Yahweh is the Lord of time and eternity, which is ultimately also expressed in Yahweh's miraculous transformation of life (Isa 35:5–6, 42:7, 61:1–3) and in his power over death (Isa 25:8). The wide variety of interpretations of and metaphors for the experience of and the hope in Yahweh as God of life found in the received form of the Old Testament goes back religio-historically to a successive expansion of Yahweh's competencies.[233] Significant factors in this process include the development of monotheism, a theology of creation that is consistent with monotheism, as well as the question of divine justice raised by the suffering of the righteous. Thus, the images of a new creation after death (Ezek 37:1–14), resurrection and reawakening (Isa 26:19),[234] immediate rapture by God beyond the boundary of death (Ps 73:24),[235] the immortality of the soul (Ps 49:16, Wis 3:1), or the ultimate defeat of death (Isa 25:8, cf. 1 Cor 15:26), which have different traditio-historical origins, are juxtaposed and merged in the notion that God's nature is revealed in God's act of giving life (Rom 4:17, cf. Wis 11:26).

The New Testament's descriptions of the post-crucifixion fate of Jesus, who according to an early Christian tradition became the son of God precisely through his divinely-ordained overcoming of death,[236] draw on these images and focus them (once again through an adaptation of Isa 52:13–53:12) on the possibility of life after death by participating through faith in the resurrection of Jesus Christ (John 3:15, cf. Rom 8:17).

---

233. Janowski, "Der Gott Israels," 112–125.
234. Cf. Dan 12:1–3, Job 42:17 LXX, 2 Macc 7:9, 4Q385 2.
235. Cf. Gen 5:22–24, 2 Kgs 2:3, 5.
236. Cf. Rom 1:3–4 with Wis 2:18, 5:5.

In this way, the Old Testament's forms of experiencing divine presence—the Sabbath (Exod 31:13–17, Ps 92), the temple (Ps 36:9–10), the Torah (Deut 30:16, Sir 24:23), and Wisdom (Prov 3:18, Sir 24)—were modified Christologically. In mythic terms, Jesus Christ thus appears as a new means of accessing the tree of life (Gen 3:24) and indeed as life itself (John 11:25).

4.7. God as the Lord of Wisdom: Jesus Christ as Reflected in Old Testament Conceptions of Wisdom

In certain respects, the conceptions of Wisdom in the Old Testament, which in their older forms are strongly oriented toward the present, stand squarely against the Old Testament's theologies of history. Operating on the assumption that God, as the creator, established a just cosmic order in this world, which the wise person can participate in through precise observation of social and natural processes and by handing down empirically-derived knowledge, the Wisdom books of the Old Testament develop their ethical program of a well-ordered life. Coupled with the notion that human actions always have consequences that extend beyond the individual and that actions and consequences are linked, this not only leads to an all-encompassing program for life but also to a social and religious distinction between the wise and fools, between the righteous and the wicked. Through individual sayings, parables, didactic speeches, and beatitudes,[237] the wise teacher seeks to lead the student to a successful life and to fear God (Prov 3:13–18). The knowledge of divinely placed limitations and of God's unknowability define the wise person just as much as the capacity to differentiate phenomena precisely and to describe reality through proverbial sayings, which always contain an implicit or explicit ethical demand.

When the theory that the wise person will prosper on account of his or her wisdom and that the righteous person should be spared from suffering on account of his or her piety is contradicted by experience, as in the case of Job, then thought governed by the act-consequence nexus is thrown into crisis. Here the utility of Wisdom is profoundly questioned (cf. Qohelet 7). The fundamental theological conception of God as the just creator becomes destabilized (Job 3, 10). Now it is no longer only the plaintive questioning of the reasons for God's hiddenness (cf. Ps 13:2, 22:2); rather, God per se becomes distant, such as in Qohelet, or God takes on malevolent traits, such as in Job (cf. Job 7, 9, 16, 19). Such a God in crisis stands in opposition to the righteous sufferer, who is exposed to suffering precisely on account of his or her righteousness before God and other people

---

237. On this, see Lichtenberger, "Makarismen in den Qumrantexten."

(Job 1:8–9), who explains his or her suffering as a divinely-ordained lesson (Job 5:17, 36:8–15, Ps 118:18), or who is proved to be righteous in and through his or her suffering (Wis 2:12–20). What is common to the different sapiential figurations of the righteous sufferer in the Old Testament, whether Job, the supplicants of Pss 35, 69, and 73, or in Wis 2–3, is the notion that suffering is not a sign of divine absence but is instead—as in the case of Jeremiah's suffering or of the suffering servant[238]—understood as a sign of unusual closeness to God, whose nature as creator and teacher is confirmed (Wis 3:1–9). The particular contribution of this critical form of Wisdom originating in the Hellenistic period is that it integrates suffering into the divine order of creation.

The books of Ben Sira and Wisdom of Solomon from the late Hellenistic and Roman periods are in a certain sense the counterpoint to this critical form of Wisdom represented by the books of Job and Qohelet, presenting a form of Wisdom that incorporates historical and eschatological thinking (Sir 44–49, Wis 10–19), teaches that evil is the necessary counterpart to good (Sir 33:7–15, taking up ideas from Stoicism),[239] makes a connection to the Torah inasmuch as the latter is understood as an incarnation of cosmic wisdom (Sir 24)[240] and even posits the immortality of the righteous sufferer (Wis 2–3). Building upon Deuteronomistic and Deutero-Isaianic concepts, this late form of Wisdom casts God as the one and only God who through divine Wisdom—which is embodied in the Torah as the law of life (Sir 17:11 LXX, 45:5)[241]—sustains the world and shows the righteous the way to life both before and beyond death, since God loves life (Wis 11:26).

The image of God that emerges from the sayings, parables, and beatitudes; the stylization of Jesus as the suffering servant, as the wise teacher, and as divine Wisdom that calls its students to life (Matt 11:28–30, Luke 7:34–35, 1 Cor 1:30);[242] Jesus' role in God's hidden plan (Rom 11:33–36); and the motif of Jesus' preexistence (1 Cor 8:6, John 1:18) are based in large part on the Old Testament's conception of God as the Lord of Wisdom, which is itself deeply rooted in concepts of order and justice attested in the ancient world from Egypt to Mesopotamia and Greece.[243]

---

238. See §4.6.2 above (p. 97).
239. Cf. Wicke-Reuter, *Göttliche Providenz*, 36–38, 273.
240. Cf. Marböck, *Weisheit im Wandel*, 34–96; Marböck, *Gottes Weisheit*, 73–87; Janowski, "Gottes Weisheit in Jerusalem," 1–29.
241. Cf. Witte, "'Das Gesetz des Lebens,'" 109–21.
242. On this, see also Schimanowski, *Weisheit und Messias*, 313–14; Oeming, "Salomo-Christologie," 74–76.
243. See p. 43.

5. Conclusion

The New Testament describes the life, death, and resurrection of Jesus Christ as part (and sometimes as the focal point and goal) of the history of God's actions toward the world and humanity. In doing so, it makes use of Old Testament and extracanonical early Jewish names, images, motifs, models of thought, and narrative structures. Old Testament scholarship illuminates the literary and religio-historical background of these elements and situates them within the history of God's actions as narrated and reflected upon in the Old Testament, which becomes a detailed prehistory of Jesus Christ. This is *not* limited to the New Testament's titles for and descriptions of Jesus' role as prophet, king, Son of David, Son of Man, Chosen One, or Messiah but instead encompasses the variety of God's life-giving actions in space and time.

Thus, the *theological* question of Jesus Christ necessarily leads to the question of the nature and development of God in the Old Testament; to reflection over God's role as creator and as director of history by accompanying, freeing, teaching, and sanctifying his people; as well as to the interpretation of metaphors for God's wisdom, kingship, and role as shepherd and father, which also took on significance in the New Testament. Christology thus requires a presentation of the basic theologies *in* the Old Testament and of a theology *of* the Old Testament. The history of Yahweh that emerges in the Old Testament and the theologies of creation, history, law, the cult, and wisdom collected therein—which, from the perspective of the New Testament, find their goal (τέλος) in the spatial-temporal focus and embodiment of God's actions through Jesus Christ—thus contribute to the history of God in the New Testament, to the discourse on Jesus Christ, and to a biblical theology.

Bibliography

Accordance® Bible Software. Version 11.2.5. OakTree Software, Inc., 2016/17.

Adrom, Faried, and Matthias Müller. "Das Tetragramm in ägyptischen Quellen: eine Bestandsaufnahme." *BTZ* 30 (2013) 120–41.

Albani, Matthias. *Der eine Gott und die himmlischen Heerscharen: Zur Begründung des Monotheismus bei Deuterojesaja im Horizont der Astralisierung des Gottesverständnisses im Alten Orient.* Arbeiten zur Bibel und ihrer Geschichte 1. Leipzig: Evangelische Verlagsanstalt, 2000.

Albertz, Rainer. *Religionsgeschichte Israels in alttestamentlicher Zeit*, vol. 1. GAT 8/1. 2nd ed. Göttingen: Vandenhoeck & Ruprecht, 1996.

Albright, William Foxwell. "The Names *SHADDAI* and *ABRAM*." *JBL* 54 (1935) 173–204.

Alt, Albrecht. *Der Gott der Väter: Ein Beitrag zur Vorgeschichte der israelitischen Religion.* BWANT 48. Stuttgart: Kohlhammer, 1929.

Altripp, Michael. "Isaac (Patriarch). VII. Visual Arts." *EBR* 13: 280–84.

Ammann, Sonja. *Götter für die Toren: Die Verbindung von Götterpolemik und Weisheit im Alten Testament.* BZAW 466. Berlin: de Gruyter, 2015.

Arneth, Martin. *"Sonne der Gerechtigkeit": Studien zur Solarisierung der Jahwe-Religion im Lichte von Psalm 72.* BZABR 1. Wiesbaden: Harrassowitz, 2000.

Arnim, Johannes von. *Stoicorum Veterum Fragmenta.* 3 vols. Stuttgart: Teubner, 1903–5.

Assmann, Jan. "Ägypten: Die Idee vom Totengericht und das Problem der Gerechtigkeit." Pp. 10–19 in *Gerechtigkeit: Richten und Retten in der abendländischen Tradition und ihren altorientalischen Ursprüngen.* Edited by Jan Assmann, Bernd Janowski, and Michael Welker. Munich: Wilhelm Fink, 1998.

_____. *Ma'at: Gerechtigkeit und Unsterblichkeit im Alten Ägypten.* 2nd ed. Munich: Beck, 1995.

Aune, David E. *Revelation 1–5.* WBC 52. Nashville: Nelson, 1997.

Bachmann, Michael. *Göttliche Allmacht und theologische Vorsicht: Zu Rezeption, Funktion und Konnotation des biblisch-frühchristlichen Gottesepithetons pantokrator.* SBS 188. Stuttgart: Katholisches Bibelwerk, 2002.

Baldermann, Ingo, ed. *Jahrbuch für Biblische Theologie*, vol. 12: *Biblische Hermeneutik.* Neukirchen-Vluyn: Neukirchener, 1997.

Barr, James. *The Concept of Biblical Theology: An Old Testament Perspective.* Philadelphia: Augsburg Fortress, 1999.

Barton, John. "The Messiah in Old Testament Theology." Pp. 365–79 in *King and Messiah in Israel and the Ancient Near East.* Edited by John Day. JSOTSup 270. Sheffield: 1998.

Baudissin, Wilhelm Wolf von. "Der gerechte Gott in altsemitischer Religion."
    Pp. 1–23 in *Festgabe von Fachgenossen und Freunden Adolf von Harnack zum
    siebzigsten Geburtstag dargebracht*. Tübingen: Mohr Siebeck, 1921.
_____. *Kyrios als Gottesname im Judentum und seine Stelle in der Religionsge-
    schichte*. 4 vols. Edited by Otto Eissfeldt. Giessen: Töpelmann, 1929.
Bauer, Walter. *Griechisch-deutsches Wörterbuch zu den Schriften des Neuen Testa-
    ments und der frühchristlichen Literatur*. Edited by Kurt Aland and Barbara
    Aland. 6th ed. Berlin: de Gruyter, 1988.
Bauks, Michaela. "The Theological Implications of Child Sacrifice in and beyond
    the Biblical Context in Relation to Genesis 22 and Judges 11." Pp. 65–86
    in *Human Sacrifice in Jewish and Christian Tradition*. Edited by Karin Fin-
    sterbusch, Armin Lange, and K. F. Diethard Römheld. Numen 112. Leiden:
    Brill, 2007.
Beck, Martin. "Messiaserwartung in den Geschichtsbüchern? Bemerkungen zur
    Funktion des Hannaliedes (I Sam 2,1–10) in seinen diversen literarischen
    Kontexten (vgl. Ex 15; Dtn 32; II Sam 22)." Pp. 231–51 in *Auf dem Weg zur
    Endgestalt von Genesis bis II Regum: Festschrift für Hans-Christoph Schmitt*.
    Edited by Martin Beck and Ulrike Schorn. BZAW 370. Berlin: de Gruyter,
    2006.
Becker, Uwe. "Psalm 72 und der Alte Orient. Grenzen und Chancen eines Ver-
    gleichs." Pp. 123–40 in *Mensch und König: Studien zur Anthropologie des Al-
    ten Testaments. Festschrift für Rüdiger Lux*. Edited by Angelika Berlejung and
    Raik Heckl. HBS 53. Freiburg: Herder, 2008.
Bedenbender, Andreas. "Als Mose und Henoch zusammenfanden. Die Entstehung
    der frühjüdischen Apokalyptik in Reaktion auf die Religionsverfolgung unter
    Antiochos IV. Epiphanes." Pp. 182–203 in *Jüdische Schriften in ihrem antik-
    jüdischen und urchristlichen Kontext*. Edited by Hermann Lichtenberger and
    Gerbern S. Oegema. JSHRZSup 1. Gütersloh: Gütersloher, 2002.
Beentjes, P. C. "Theodicy in the Wisdom of Ben Sira." Pp. 509–24 in *Theodicy
    in the World of the Bible*. Edited by Antti Laato and Johannes C. de Moor.
    Leiden: Brill, 2003.
Berner, Christoph. "'I am Yhwh your God, who brought you out of the land of
    Egypt' (Exod 20:2): Reflections on the Status of the Exodus Creed in the
    History of Israel and the Literary History of the Hebrew Bible." Pp. 181–206
    in *The Origins of Yahwism*. Edited by Jürgen van Oorschot and Markus Witte.
    BZAW 484. Berlin: de Gruyter, 2017.
Bertram, Georg. "ΙΚΑΝΟΣ in den griechischen Übersetzungen des ATs als Wie-
    dergabe von *schaddaj*." *ZAW* 70 (1958) 20–31.
_____. "Zur Prägung der biblischen Gottesvorstellung in der griechischen Über-
    setzung des Alten Testaments: Die Wiedergabe von schadad und schaddaj im
    Griechischen." Pp. 211–213 in *Akten des vierundzwanzigsten Internation-
    alen Orientalisten-Kongresses Munich 1957*. Edited by H. Franke. Wiesbaden:
    Steiner, 1959.
Bezzel, Hannes. *Die Konfessionen Jeremias: Eine redaktionsgeschichtliche Studie*.
    BZAW 378. Berlin: de Gruyter, 2007.

Biblia Hebraica Stuttgartensia. Edited by Karl Elliger and Wilhelm Rudolph. 5th edition. Edited by Adrian Schenker. Stuttgart: Deutsche Bibelgesellschaft, 1997.

Blum, Erhard. "Die Kombination I der Wandinschrift vom Tell Deir ʿAlla. Vorschläge zur Rekonstruktion mit historisch-kritischen Anmerkungen." Pp. 573–601 in *Berührungspunkte: Festschrift für Rainer Albertz.* Edited by Ingo Kottsieper, Rüdiger Schmitt, and Jakob Wöhrle. AOAT 350. Münster: Ugarit-Verlag, 2008.

_____. " 'Verstehst du dich nicht auf die Schreibkunst. . . ?' Ein weisheitlicher Dialog über Vergänglichkeit und Verantwortung: Kombination II der Wandinschrift vom Tell Deir ʿAlla." Pp. 33–53 in *Was ist der Mensch, dass du seiner gedenkst? (Psalm 8,5): Festschrift für Bernd Janowski.* Edited by Michaela Bauks, Kathrin Liess, and Peter Riede. Neukirchen-Vluyn: Neukirchener, 2008.

Boccaccini, Gabriele. *Enoch and the Messiah Son of Man: Revisiting the Book of Parables.* Grand Rapids: Eerdmans, 2007.

Bornkamm, Heinrich. *Luther und das Alte Testament.* Tübingen: Mohr Siebeck, 1948.

Bousset, Wilhelm, and Hugo Gressmann. *Die Religion des Judentums im späthellenistischen Zeitalter.* HNT 21. 3rd ed. Tübingen: Mohr Siebeck, 1926.

Brandt, Peter. *Endgestalten des Kanons: Das Arrangement der Schriften Israels in der jüdischen und christlichen Bibel.* BBB 131. Berlin: Philo, 2001.

Breytenbach, Cilliers. "HΥΡSISTOS ὁ ὕψιστος." *DDD*[2]: 439–43.

Brown, Francis, S. R. Driver, and Charles A. Briggs. *Hebrew and English Lexicon with an Appendix containing the Biblical Aramaic.* Boston: Houghton, Mifflin & Company, 1906.

Brown, John Pairman. *Israel and Hellas.* 3 vols. BZAW 231, 276, 299. Berlin: de Gruyter, 1995, 2000, 2001.

Brueggemann, Walter. *Theology of the Old Testament: Testimony, Dispute, Advocacy.* Minneapolis: Fortress, 1997.

Bultmann, Rudolf. "Weissagung und Erfüllung." Pp. 231–55 in *Gesammelte Aufsätze.* Edited by Karl Matthiae. Berlin: Evangelische Verlagsanstalt, 1973.

Campenhausen, Hans Freiherr von. *Die Entstehung der christlichen Bibel.* BHT 39. Tübingen: Mohr Siebeck, 1968.

Cazelles, Henri. *Alttestamentliche Christologie: Zur Geschichte der Messiasidee.* Theologia Romanica 13. Einsiedeln: Johannes, 1983.

Charlesworth, James H., ed. *The Old Testament Pseudepigrapha.* 2 vols. New York: Doubleday, 1983, 1985.

_____, ed. *The Messiah: Developments in Earliest Judaism and Christianity.* Minneapolis: Fortress, 1992.

Charlesworth, James H., Hermann Lichtenberger, and Gerbern S. Oegema, eds. *Qumran Messianism: Studies on the Messianic Expectations in the Dead Sea Scrolls.* Tübingen: Mohr Siebeck, 1998.

Cheney, Michael. *Dust, Wind, and Agony: Character, Speech and Genre in Job,* ConBibOTS 36. Lund: Almqvist & Wiksell, 1994.

Childs, Brevard S. *Biblical Theology of the Old and New Testaments*. London: SCM, 1992.

_____. *Introduction to the Old Testament as Scripture*. London: SCM, 1979.

Clements, Ronald E. *Old Testament Theology: A Fresh Approach*. London: Marshall, Morgan & Scott, 1978.

Clines, David J. A. *Job 1–20*. WBC 17. Dallas: Word, 1989.

Clines, David J. A., ed. *The Concise Dictionary of Classical Hebrew*. Sheffield: Sheffield Academic Press, 2009.

_____. *The Dictionary of Classical Hebrew*. 8 vols. Sheffield: Sheffield Academic Press, 1993–2011.

Cohen, Hermann. *Religion der Vernunft aus den Quellen des Judentums: Eine jüdische Religionsphilosophie*. Darmstadt: Joseph Melzer, 1966.

Collins, Adela Yarbro, and John J. Collins. *King and Messiah as Son of God: Divine, Human, and Angelic Messianic Figures in Biblical and Related Literature*. Grand Rapids: Eerdmans, 2008.

Collins, John J. *The Apocalyptic Imagination: An Introduction to Jewish Apocalyptic Literature*. 2nd ed. Grand Rapids: Eerdmans, 1998.

_____. *The Scepter and the Star: The Messiahs of the Dead Sea Scrolls and Other Ancient Literature*. New York: Doubleday, 1995.

Cook, Arthur Bernhard. *Zeus: A Study in Ancient Religion*, vols. 2/2 and 3. Cambridge: Cambridge University Press, 1925, 1940.

Cowley, Arthur Ernest. *Aramaic Papyri of the Fifth Century B.C., Edited, with Translation and Notes*. Oxford: Clarendon, 1923.

Cross, Frank Moore. *Canaanite Myth and Hebrew Epic: Essays in the History of the Religion of Israel*. Cambridge: Harvard University Press, 1973.

Crüsemann, Frank. *Das Alte Testament als Wahrheitsraum des Neuen: Die neue Sicht der christlichen Bibel*. Gütersloh: Gütersloher, 2011.

_____. *Der Widerstand gegen das Königtum: Die antiköniglichen Texte des Alten Testaments und der Kampf um den frühen israelitischen Staat*. WMANT 49. Neukirchen-Vluyn: Neukirchener, 1978.

_____. *Die Tora: Theologie und Sozialgeschichte des alttestamentlichen Gesetzes*. Munich: Chr. Kaiser, 1992.

_____. "Jahwes Gerechtigkeit (ṣᵉdāqāh/ṣädäq)." *EvTh* 36 (1976) 427–50.

Davies, G. I. *Ancient Hebrew Inscriptions: Corpus and Concordance*. 2 vols. New York: Cambridge University Press, 1991, 2004.

Day, John, ed. *King and Messiah in Israel and the Ancient Near East*. JSOTSup 270. Sheffield: Sheffield Academic, 1998.

Deichmann, Friedrich-Wilhelm, ed. *Repertorium der christlich-antiken Sarkophage*, Bd. 1, *Rom und Ostia, Textband und Tafelband*. Wiesbaden: Steiner, 1967.

Delcor, Mathias. "Des inscriptions de Deir ʿAlla aux traditions bibliques, à propos des šdyn, des šēdîm et de šadday." Pp. 33–40 in *Die Väter Israels: Beiträge zur Theologie der Patriarchenüberlieferung im Alten Testament: Festschrift für Josef Scharbert*. Edited by Manfred Görg. Stuttgart: Katholisches Bibelwerk, 1989.

Delitzsch, Friedrich. *Die Grosse Täuschung*. 2 vols. Lorch: Karl Rohm, 1924, 1926.

_____. *Prolegomena eines neuen hebräisch-aramäischen Wörterbuchs zum Alten Testament*. Leipzig: Hinrichs, 1886.

Denis, Albert-Marie. *Concordance Grecque des Pseudépigraphes d'Ancien Testament: Concordance, corpus des textes, indices.* Louvain-la-Neuve: Université Catholique de Louvain, 1987.

_____, ed. *Fragmenta Pseudepigraphorum quae supersunt graeca una cum historicorum et auctorum Judaeorum hellenistarum fragmentis.* PVTG IIIb. Leiden: Brill, 1970.

Dietrich, Manfried, Oswald Loretz, and Joaqín Sanmartín. *The Cuneiform Alphabetic Texts from Ugarit, Ras Ibn Hani and Other Places (KTU: second, enlarged edition).* Abhandlungen zur Literatur Alt-Syrien-Palästinas und Mesopotamiens 8. Münster: Ugarit-Verlag, 1995.

Dietrich, Walter. "Der rote Faden im Alten Testament." Pp. 13–18 in *"Theopolitik": Studien zur Theologie und Ethik des Alten Testaments.* Neukirchen-Vluyn: Neukirchener, 2002.

Diogenes Laertius. *Lives of Eminent Philosophers.* 2 vols. Trans. Robert D. Hicks. LCL 184. London: Heinemann, 1925.

Dohmen, Christoph. "Hermeneutik, II. AT." *RGG*⁴ 3: 1649–51.

Dohmen, Christoph, and Günter Stemberger. *Hermeneutik der Jüdischen Bibel und des Alten Testaments.* KStTh 1/2. Stuttgart: Kohlhammer, 1996.

Donner, Herbert, and Wolfgang Röllig. *Kanaanäische und aramäische Inschriften,* vol. 1. 5th ed. Wiesbaden: Harrassowitz, 2002.

Ego, Beate, Armin Lange, and Peter Pilhofer, eds. *Gemeinde ohne Tempel.* WUNT 119. Tübingen: Mohr Siebeck, 1999.

Eichrodt, Walter. *Theologie des Alten Testaments.* 3 vols. Leipzig: Hinrichs, 1933, 1935, 1939.

Engelmann, Helmut. *Die Inschriften von Ephesos: Teil 4: Nr. 1001–1445.* Inschriften griechischer Städte aus Kleinasien 14. Bonn: Habelt, 1980.

Enns, Peter. *Ecclesiastes.* The Two Horizons Old Testament Commentary. Grand Rapids: Eerdmans, 2011.

Erman, Adolf, and Hermann Grapow. *Wörterbuch der ägyptischen Sprache.* 6 vols. Berlin: Akademie, 1937–55.

Evans, Craig A. "Messiahs." *EDSS* 2: 537–42.

Fabry, Heinz-Josef and Klaus Scholtissek. *Der Messias: Perspektiven des Alten und Neuen Testaments.* NEchtB. Themen 5. Würzburg: Echter, 2002.

Fabry, Heinz-Josef and Helmer Ringgren, eds. *Theologisches Wörterbuch zum Alten Testament.* 10 vols. Stuttgart: Kohlhammer, 1973–1995.

Fauth, Wolfgang. *Helios Megistos: Zur synkretistischen Theologie der Spätantike.* Religions in the Graeco-Roman World 125. Leiden: Brill, 1995.

Felber, Stefan. *Wilhelm Vischer als Ausleger der heiligen Schrift: Eine Untersuchung zum Christuszeugnis des Alten Testaments.* FSÖTh 89. Göttingen: Vandenhoeck & Ruprecht, 1999.

Feldmeier, Reinhard. "Almighty παντοκράτωρ." *DDD*²: 20–23.

_____. "Nicht Übermacht noch Impotenz. Zum biblischen Ursprung des Allmachtsbekenntnisses." Pp. 13–42 in *Der Allmächtige: Annäherungen an ein umstrittenes Gottesprädikat.* Edited by Werner H. Ritter et al. BTSP 13. Göttingen: Vandenhoeck & Ruprecht, 1997.

Feldmeier, Reinhard and Hermann Spieckermann. *Der Gott der Lebendigen: Eine biblische Gotteslehre*. Topoi Biblischer Theologie 1. Tübingen: Mohr Siebeck, 2011.

Finkelstein, Israel, and Neil Asher Silberman. *The Bible Unearthed: Archaeology's New Vision of Ancient Israel and the Origin of Its Sacred Texts*. New York: Free Press, 2001.

Fohrer, Georg. "Das Alte Testament und das Thema 'Christologie'." *EvTh 30* (1970) 281–98.

_____. *Das Buch Hiob*. KAT XVI. 2nd ed. Gütersloh: Gütersloher, 1989.

Franz, Matthias. *Der barmherzige und gnädige Gott: Die Gnadenrede vom Sinai (Exodus 34,6–7) und ihre Parallelen im Alten Testament und seiner Umwelt*. BWANT 160. Stuttgart: Kohlhammer, 2003.

Freedman, H., and Maurice Simon. *Midrash Rabbah translated into English with notes, glossary and indices in ten volumes: Genesis in two volumes*. London: Soncino, 1961.

Frey, Jörg. "Die Textfunde von Qumran und die neutestamentliche Wissenschaft." Pp. 225–93 in *Qumran aktuell: Text und Themen der Schriften vom Toten Meer*. Edited by Stefan Beyerle and Jörg Frey. BThSt 120. Neukirchen-Vluyn: Neukirchener, 2011.

Furley, William D., and Jan Maarten Bremer. *Greek Hymns*, vol. 1: *The Texts in Translation*. Studien zu Antike und Christentum 9. Tübingen: Mohr Siebeck, 2001; vol. 2: *Greek Texts and Commentary*. Studien zu Antike und Christentum 10. Tübingen: Mohr Siebeck, 2001.

García Martínez, Florentino, and Eibert J. C. Tigchelaar, eds. *The Dead Sea Scrolls: Study Edition*. 2 vols. Leiden: Brill, 1997, 1998.

Gauger, Jörg-Dieter. *Sibyllinische Weissagungen: Griechisch-deutsch: Auf der Grundlage der Ausgabe von Alfons Kurfeß neu übersetzt und herausgegeben*. Sammlung Tusculum. 2nd ed. Düsseldorf: Artemis, 2002.

Gentry, Peter J. *The Asterisked Materials in the Greek Job*. SBLSCS 38. Atlanta: Scholars Press, 1995.

Gertz, Jan Christian. *Tradition und Redaktion in der Exoduserzählung: Untersuchungen zur Endredaktion des Pentateuch*. FRLANT 186. Göttingen: Vandenhoeck & Ruprecht, 2000.

_____. "Von Adam zu Enosch: Überlegungen zur Entstehungsgeschichte von Genesis 2–4." Pp. 215–36 in *Gott und Mensch im Dialog: Festschrift für Otto Kaiser*. Edited by Markus Witte. BZAW 345/1. Berlin: de Gruyter, 2004.

Gertz, Jan Christian et al. *T&T Clark Handbook of the Old Testament: An Introduction to the Literature, Religion and History of the Old Testament*. London: T. & T. Clark, 2012.

Gese, Hartmut. "Erwägungen zur Einheit der biblischen Theologie." Pp. 11–30 in *Vom Sinai zum Zion: Alttestamentliche Beiträge zur biblischen Theologie*. BEvTh 64. Munich: Chr. Kaiser, 1974.

_____. "Τὸ δὲ Ἀγὰρ Σινὰ ὄρος ἐστὶν ἐν τῇ Ἀραβίᾳ (Gal 4,25)." Pp. 49–62 in *Vom Sinai zum Zion: Alttestamentliche Beiträge zur biblischen Theologie*. BEvTh 64. Munich: Chr. Kaiser, 1974.

Gesenius, Wilhelm. *Hebräisches und Aramäisches Handwörterbuch über das Alte Testament*. Edited by Frants Buhl. 17th ed. Leipzig: Vogel, 1915.

_____. *Hebräisches und Aramäisches Handwörterbuch über das Alte Testament*. Edited by Herbert Donner. 18th ed. Berlin: Springer, 2013.

_____. *Thesaurus philologicus criticus linguae Hebraeae et Chaldaeae Veteris Testamenti: Editio altera secundum radices digesta priore germanica longe auctior et emendatior*. 3 vols. Leipzig: Vogel, 1829–42.

Gesundheit, Shimon. "'Gibt es eine jüdische Theologie der hebräischen Bibel?'" Pp. 73–86 in *Theologie und Exegese des Alten Testaments / der Hebräischen Bibel: Zwischenbilanz und Zukunftsperspektiven*. Edited by Bernd Janowski. SBS 200. Stuttgart: Katholisches Bibelwerk, 2005.

Glatzer, Nahum N. "The God of Job and the God of Abraham. Some Talmudic-Midrashic Interpretations of the Book of Job." *BIJS* 2 (1974) 41–57.

Goff, Matthew. *Discerning Wisdom: The Sapiential Literature of the Dead Sea Scrolls*. VTSup 116. Leiden: Brill, 2007.

Goldschmidt, Lazarus. תלמוד בבלי. *Der Babylonische Talmud: Nach der ersten zensurfreien Ausgabe unter Berücksichtigung der neueren Ausg. und handschriftlichen Materials neu übertragen*. 12 vols. 2nd ed. Berlin: Jüdischer Verlag, 1964–67.

Görg, Manfred. "Šaddaj—Ehrenrettung einer Etymologie." *BN* 16 (1981) 13–15.

_____. "Schaddai." *NBL* 3: 454–55.

Gowan, Donald E. *Eschatology in the Old Testament*. 2nd ed. London: T. & T. Clark, 2000.

Granerød, Gard. *Dimensions of Yahwism in the Persian Period: Studies in the Religion and Society of the Judaean Community at Elephantine*. BZAW 488. Berlin: de Gruyter, 2016.

Gunneweg, Antonius Hermanus Josephus. *Vom Verstehen des Alten Testaments*. GAT 5. 2nd ed. Göttingen: Vandenhoeck & Ruprecht, 1988.

Hallo, William W., ed. *The Context of Scripture*. 3 vols. Leiden: Brill, 1997, 2000, 2002.

Hartenstein, Friedhelm. *Das Angesicht JHWHs: Studien zu seinem höfischen und kultischen Bedeutungshintergrund in den Psalmen und in Exodus 32–34*. FAT 55. Tübingen: Mohr Siebeck, 2008.

_____. "Die Geschichte JHWHs im Spiegel seiner Namen." Pp. 73–95 in *Gott nennen: Gottes Namen und Gott als Name*. Edited by Ingolf U. Dalferth and Philipp Stoellger. Religion in Philosophy and Theology 35. Tübingen: Mohr Siebeck, 2008.

_____. "Wettergott—Schöpfergott—Einziger. Kosmologie und Monotheismus in den Psalmen." Pp. 77–97 in *JHWH und die Götter der Völker*. Edited by Friedhelm Hartenstein and Martin Rösel. Neukirchen-Vluyn: Neukirchener, 2009.

Hempel, Johannes. "Gottesgedanke und Rechtsgestaltung in Altisrael." *ZSTh* 8/2 (1930) 377–395.

Hengel, Martin. *Judentum und Hellenismus: Studien zu ihrer Begegnung unter besonderer Berücksichtigung Palästinas bis zur Mitte des 2. Jh.s. v.Chr.* WUNT 10. 3rd ed. Tübingen: Mohr Siebeck, 1988.

Hirsch, Emanuel. *Das Alte Testament und die Predigt des Evangeliums*. Tübingen: Mohr Siebeck, 1936.

Hirsch, Samson Raphael. *Der Pentateuch*, vol. 1: *Die Genesis*. Tel Aviv: Sinai Publishing, 1986.

Hoffmann, Friedhelm, and Joachim Friedrich Quack. *Anthologie der Demotischen Literatur*. Einführungen und Quellentexte zur Ägyptologie 4. Münster: LIT, 2007.

Hofius, Otfried. "Ist Jesus der Messias?" Pp. 103–29 in *Der Messias: Jahrbuch für Biblische Theologie*, vol. 8. Edited by Ingo Baldermann. Neukirchen-Vluyn: Neukirchener, 1993.

Hoftijzer, J., and K. Jongeling. *Dictionary of the North-West Semitic Inscriptions*. 2 vols. HdO I/21. Leiden: Brill, 1995.

Hommel, Hildebrecht. "Pantokrator" [1954/56]. Pp. 131–77 in *Sebasmata: Studien zur antiken Religionsgeschichte und zum frühen Christentum*, vol. 1. WUNT 31. Tübingen: Mohr Siebeck, 1983.

Horn, Friedrich-Wilhelm. "Ortsverschiebungen. Transformationen des Gottesverständnisses im Neuen Testament." Pp. 69–82 in *Gott—Götter—Götzen*. Edited by Christoph Schwöbel. VWGTh 38. Leipzig: Evangelische Verlagsanstalt, 2013.

Horsley, G. H. R. *New Documents Illustrating Early Christianity*, vol. 3: *A Review of the Greek Inscriptions and Papyri Published 1978*. North Ryde: Macquarie University, 1983.

Horst, Friedrich. "Gerechtigkeit Gottes, II. Im AT und Judentum." *RGG*³ 2: 1403–6.

Houtman, Cees. *Der Pentateuch: Die Geschichte seiner Erforschung neben einer Auswertung*. CBET 9. Kampen: Kok Pharos, 1994.

Hübner, Hans. *Vetus Testamentum in Novo*, vol. 1/2: *Evangelium Johannis*. Göttingen: Vandenhoeck & Ruprecht, 2003.

_____. *Vetus Testamentum in Novo*, vol. 2: *Corpus Paulinum*. Göttingen: Vandenhoeck & Ruprecht, 1997.

Hutter, Manfred. *Religionen in der Umwelt des Alten Testaments I: Babylonier, Syrer, Perser*. KStTh 4,1. Stuttgart: Kohlhammer, 1996.

Jacobs, Irving. *The Midrashic Process: Tradition and Interpretation in Rabbinic Judaism*, Cambridge: Cambridge University Press, 1995.

Janowski, Bernd. "Biblische Theologie. I. Exegetisch." *RGG*⁴ 1: 1544–49.

_____. "Der barmherzige Richter. Zur Einheit von Gerechtigkeit und Barmherzigkeit im Gottesbild des Alten Orients." Pp. 75–133 in *Der Gott des Lebens: Beiträge zur Theologie des Alten Testaments 3*. Neukirchen-Vluyn: Neukirchener, 2003.

_____. "Der Gott Israels und die Toten: Eine religions- und theologiegeschichtliche Skizze." Pp. 99–138 in *JHWH und die Götter der Völker*. Edited by Friedhelm Hartenstein and Martin Rösel, Neukirchen: Neukirchener, 2009.

_____. "Der Gute Hirte: Psalm 23 und das biblische Gottesbild." Pp. 247–71 in *Ex oriente Lux: Studien zur Theologie des Alten Testaments: Festschrift für Rüdiger Lux*. Edited by Angelika Berlejung and Raik Heckl. Arbeiten zur Bibel und ihrer Geschichte 39. Leipzig: Evangelische Verlagsanstalt, 2012.

_____. "Israel: Der göttliche Richter und seine Gerechtigkeit." Pp. 20–28 in *Gerechtigkeit: Richten und Retten in der abendländischen Tradition und ihren altorientalischen Ursprüngen.* Edited by Jan Assmann, Bernd Janowski, and Michael Welker. Munich: Wilhelm Fink, 1998.

_____. "Der Ort des Lebens. Zur Kultsymbolik des Jerusalemer Tempels." Pp. 369–397 in *Temple Building and Temple Cult: Architecture and Cultic Paraphernalia of Temples in the Levant (2.–1. Mill. BCE).* Edited by Jens Kamlah and Henrike Michelau. ADPV 41. Wiesbaden: Harrassowitz, 2012.

_____. "Die Frucht der Gerechtigkeit. Psalm 72 und die judäische Königsideologie." Pp. 94–134 in *"Mein Sohn bist du" (Ps 2,7). Studien zu den Königspsalmen.* Edited by Eckart Otto and Erich Zenger. SBS 192. Stuttgart: Katholisches Bibelwerk, 2002.

_____. "Gottes Weisheit in Jerusalem. Sirach 24 und die biblische Schekina-Theologie." Pp. 1–29 in *Biblical Figures in Deuterocanonical and Cognate Literature.* Edited by Hermann Lichtenberger and Ulrike Mittmann-Richert. Deuterocanonical and Cognate Literature Yearbook 2008. Berlin: de Gruyter, 2009.

_____. "JHWH der Richter—ein rettender Gott: Psalm 7 und das Motiv des Gottesgerichts." Pp. 92–124 in *Die rettende Gerechtigkeit: Beiträge zur Theologie des Alten Testaments* 2. Neukirchen-Vluyn: Neukirchener, 1999.

_____. "JHWH und der Sonnengott. Aspekte der Solarisierung JHWHs in vorexilischer Zeit." Pp. 192–219 in *Die rettende Gerechtigkeit: Beiträge zur Theologie des Alten Testaments* 2. Neukirchen-Vluyn: Neukirchener, 1999.

_____, ed. *Theologie und Exegese des Alten Testaments / der Hebräischen Bibel: Zwischenbilanz und Zukunftsperspektive.* SBS 200. Stuttgart: Katholisches Bibelwerk, 2005.

Janowski, Bernd and Gernot Wilhelm, eds. *Texte aus der Umwelt des Alten Testaments: Neue Folge.* 8 vols. Gütersloh: Gütersloher, 2004–15.

Janowski, Bernd, and Peter Stuhlmacher, eds. *Der leidende Gottesknecht: Jesaja 53 und seine Wirkungsgeschichte.* FAT 14. Tübingen: Mohr Siebeck, 1996.

Jaroš, Karl. *Inschriften des Heiligen Landes aus vier Jahrtausenden.* CD-ROM. Mainz: Philipp von Zabern, 2001.

Jastrow, Marcus. *A Dictionary of the Targumim, the Talmud Babli and Yerushalmi, and the Midrashic Literature.* 2 vols. New York: Judaica, 1903.

Jeremias, Joachim. "Μωυσῆς." *TWNT* 4: 852–78.

Jeremias, Jörg, ed. *Gerechtigkeit und Leben im hellenistischen Zeitalter: Symposion anläßlich des 75. Geburtstags von Otto Kaiser.* BZAW 296. Berlin: de Gruyter, 2001.

Kähler, Martin. *Jesus und das Alte Testament [1907/1937]: Bearbeitet und mit einer Einführung versehen von Ernst Kähler.* BSt 45. Neukirchen-Vluyn: Neukirchener, 1965.

Kaiser, Otto. *Der eine Gott Israels und die Mächte der Welt: Der Weg Gottes im Alten Testament vom Herrn seines Volkes zum Herrn der ganzen Welt.* FRLANT 249. Göttingen: Vandenhoeck & Ruprecht, 2013.

_____. *Der Gott des Alten Testaments: Theologie des Alten Testaments: Teil 1, Grundlegung.* UTB 1747. Göttingen: Vandenhoeck & Ruprecht, 1993.

_____. *Der Gott des Alten Testaments: Wesen und Wirken: Theologie des Alten Testaments: Teil 2, Jahwe, der Gott Israels, Schöpfer der Welt und des Menschen.* UTB 2024. Göttingen: Vandenhoeck & Ruprecht, 1998.

_____. *Der Gott des Alten Testaments: Theologie des Alten Testaments, Teil 3: Jahwes Gerechtigkeit.* UTB 2392. Göttingen: Vandenhoeck & Ruprecht, 2003.

_____. "Dike und Sedaqa. Zur Frage nach der sittlichen Weltordnung. Ein theologisches Präludium." Pp. 1–23 in *Der Mensch und dem Schicksal: Studien zur Geschichte, Theologie und Gegenwartsbedeutung der Weisheit.* BZAW 161. Berlin: de Gruyter, 1985.

_____, ed. *Texte aus der Umwelt des Alten Testaments.* 3 vols. Gütersloh: Gütersloher, 1982–1997.

_____, ed. *Texte aus der Umwelt des Alten Testaments, Ergänzungsband.* Gütersloh: Gütersloher, 2001.

Karrer, Martin. *Der Gesalbte: Grundlagen des Christustitels.* FRLANT 154. Göttingen: Vandenhoeck & Ruprecht, 1998.

_____. *Jesus Christus im Neuen Testament.* GNT 11. Göttingen: Vandenhoeck & Ruprecht, 1998.

_____. "Messias / Messianismus, IV. Christentum 1. Neues Testament." *RGG*[4] 5: 1150–53.

_____. "Von David zu Christus." Pp. 327–65 in *König David: Biblische Schlüsselfigur und europäische Leitgestalt.* Edited by Walter Dietrich and Hubert Herkommer. Stuttgart: Kohlhammer, 2003.

Keel, Othmar. *Die Geschichte Jerusalems und die Entstehung des Monotheismus, Teil 1.* OLB IV/1. Göttingen: Vandenhoeck & Ruprecht, 2007.

_____. *Jahwes Entgegnung an Ijob: Eine Deutung von Ijob 38–41 vor dem Hintergrund der zeitgenössischen Bildkunst.* FRLANT 121. Göttingen: Vandenhoeck & Ruprecht, 1978.

Keel, Othmar and Christoph Uehlinger. *Göttinnen, Götter und Gottessymbole: Neue Erkenntnisse zur Religionsgeschichte Kanaans und Israels aufgrund bislang unerschlossener ikonographischer Quellen.* QD 134. Freiburg: Herder, 1992 (6th ed., 2010).

_____. *Altorientalische Miniaturkunst: Die ältesten visuellen Massenkommunikationsmittel: Ein Blick in die Sammlungen des Biblischen Instituts der Universität Freiburg Schweiz.* 2nd expanded edition. Fribourg: Universitätsverlag, 1996.

Klaiber, Walter, ed. *Biblische Grundlagen der Rechtfertigungslehre: Eine ökumenische Studie zur Gemeinsamen Erklärung zur Rechtfertigungslehre.* Leipzig: Evangelische Verlagsanstalt, 2012.

Knauf, Ernst Axel. "El Šaddaj." *BN* 16 (1981) 20–26.

_____. "SHADDAY שׁדי." *DDD*[2]: 749–53.

Knoppers, Gary N., and Bernard Levinson, eds. *The Pentateuch as Torah: New Models for Understanding Its Promulgation and Acceptance.* Winona Lake: Eisenbrauns, 2007.

Koch, Christoph. *Vertrag, Treueid und Bund: Studien zur Rezeption des altorientalischen Vertragsrechts im Deuteronomium und zur Ausbildung der Bundestheologie im Alten Testament.* BZAW 383. Berlin: de Gruyter, 2008.

Koch, Heidemarie. "Die Religion der Iraner." Pp. 80–144 in *Religionen des Alten Orients: Teil 1. Hethiter und Iran*. Edited by Volkert Haas and Heidemarie Koch. GAT 1,1. Göttingen: Vandenhoeck & Ruprecht, 2011.

Koch, Klaus. "Ṣädaq und Ma'at. Konnektive Gerechtigkeit in Israel und Ägypten?" Pp. 37–64 in *Gerechtigkeit: Richten und Retten in der abendländischen Tradition und ihren altorientalischen Ursprüngen*. Edited by Jan Assmann, Bernd Janowski, and Michael Welker. Munich: Wilhelm Fink, 1998.

_____. "ŠADDAJ. Zum Verhältnis zwischen israelitischer Monolatrie und nordwestsemitischem Polytheismus." Pp. 118–52 in *Studien zur alttestamentlichen und altorientalischen Religionsgeschichte*. Edited by Eckart Otto. Göttingen: Vandenhoeck & Ruprecht, 1986.

_____. *Von der Wende der Zeiten: Beiträge zur apokalyptischen Literatur: Gesammelte Aufsätze*, vol. 3. Neukirchen-Vluyn: Neukirchener, 1996.

Köckert, Matthias. "'Glaube' und 'Gerechtigkeit' in Gen 15,6." *ZTK* 109 (2012) 415–44.

_____. "Gott der Väter." *NBL* 1: 915–19.

_____. *Vätergott und Väterverheißungen: Eine Auseinandersetzung mit Albrecht Alt und seinen Erben*. FRLANT 142. Göttingen: Vandenhoeck & Ruprecht, 1988.

Köhler, Ludwig. *Theologie des Alten Testaments*. NTG. 2nd ed. Tübingen: Mohr Siebeck, 1947.

Köhler, Ludwig, and Walter Baumgartner. *Hebräisches und Aramäisches Lexikon zum Alten Testament*. Edited by Johann Jakob Stamm and Benedikt Hartmann. 5 vols. 3rd ed. Leiden: Brill, 1967–1995.

König, Eduard. *Hebräisches und aramäisches Wörterbuch zum Alten Testament*. 4th and 5th ed. Leipzig: Dieterisch'sche Verlagsbuchhandlung, 1931.

Kratz, Reinhard G. *Die Komposition der erzählenden Bücher des Alten Testaments: Grundwissen der Bibelkritik*. UTB 2157. Göttingen: Vandenhoeck & Ruprecht, 2000.

_____. "The Second Temple of Jeb and of Jerusalem." Pp. 247–64 in *Judah and the Judeans in the Persian Period*. Edited by Oded Lipschits and Manfred Oeming. Winona Lake, IN: Eisenbrauns, 2006.

Kraus, Hans-Joachim. *Die Biblische Theologie: Ihre Geschichte und Problematik*. Neukirchen-Vluyn: Neukirchener, 1970.

Kraus, Wolfgang, and Martin Karrer, eds. *Septuaginta Deutsch: Das griechische Alte Testament in deutscher Übersetzung*. 2nd ed. Stuttgart: Deutsche Bibelgesellschaft, 2010.

Laato, Antti. *A Star is Rising: The Historical Development of the Old Testament Royal Ideology and the Rise of the Jewish Messianic Expectations*. Atlanta: Scholars Press, 1997.

Lang, Bernhard. "Herr der Tiere." *NBL* 3: 858–72.

_____. *Jahwe: Der biblische Gott: Ein Porträt*. Munich: Beck, 2002.

Lange, Armin. "'They Burn Their Sons and Daughters—That Was No Command of Mine' (Jer 7:31)." Pp. 109–32 in *Human Sacrifice in Jewish and Christian Tradition*. Edited by Karin Finsterbusch, Armin Lange, and K. F. Diethard Römheld. Numen 112. Leiden: Brill, 2007.

Langenhorst, Georg. *Hiob unser Zeitgenosse: Die literarische Hiob-Rezeption im 20.
   Jahrhundert als theologische Herausforderung.* Theologie und Literatur 1. 2nd
   ed. Mainz: Matthias Grünewald, 1995.

Lehmann, Reinhard G. *Friedrich Delitzsch und der Babel-Bibel-Streit.* OBO 133.
   Göttingen: Vandenhoeck & Ruprecht, 1994.

Leuenberger, Martin. "Die Solarisierung des Wettergottes Jhwh." Pp. 34–71 in
   *Gott in Bewegung: Religions- und theologiegeschichtliche Beiträge zu Gottesvor-
   stellungen im alten Israel.* FAT 76. Tübingen: Mohr Siebeck, 2011.

Lévêque, Jean. *Job et son dieu.* 2 vols. ÉtB. Paris: Gabalda, 1970.

Levin, Christoph. "Altes Testament und Rechtfertigung." *ZTK* 96 (1999) 162–76.

_____. "Das Alte Testament und die Predigt des Evangeliums." *KuD* 57 (2011)
   41–55.

_____. *Der Jahwist.* FRLANT 157. Göttingen: Vandenhoeck & Ruprecht, 1993.

_____. *Die Verheißung des neuen Bundes in ihrem theologiegeschichtlichen Zusam-
   menhang ausgelegt.* FRLANT 137. Göttingen: Vandenhoeck & Ruprecht,
   1985.

Levy, Jacob. *Chaldäisches Wörterbuch über die Targumim und einen grossen Theil
   des rabbinischen Schriftthums.* 2 vols. Leipzig: Baumgärtner, 1867, 1868.

_____. *Wörterbuch über die Talmudim und Midraschim: Nebst Beiträgen v. H. L.
   Fleischer u. d: Nachträgen u: Berichtigungen zur 2. Aufl. v. L. Goldschmidt.*
   4 vols. Berlin: Harz, 1924.

Lichtenberger, Hermann. "Makarismen in den Qumrantexten und im Neuen Testament." Pp. 167–82 in *Weisheit in Israel.* Edited by David J. A. Clines, Hermann Lichtenberger, and Hans-Peter Müller. Altes Testament und Moderne
   12. Münster: LIT, 2003.

Liddell, Henry George, Robert Scott, and Henry Stuart Jones. *Greek-English Lexicon.* 9th ed., with a Revised Supplement. Oxford: Clarendon, 1996.

Lightfoot, J. L. *The Sibylline Oracles with Introduction, Translations, and Commentary on the First and Second Books.* Oxford: Oxford University Press, 2007.

Livingstone, Alasdair. *State Archives of Assyria,* vol. 3: *Court Poetry and Literary
   Miscellanea.* Helsinki: Helsinki University Press, 1989.

Liwak, Rüdiger. "Der Herrscher als Wohltäter. Soteriologische Aspekte in den
   Königstraditionen des Alten Orients und des Alten Testaments." Pp. 163–87
   in *Israel in der altorientalischen Welt: Gesammelte Studien zur Kultur und
   Religionsgeschichte des antiken Israel.* Edited by Dagmar Pruin and Markus
   Witte. BZAW 444. Berlin: de Gruyter, 2013.

_____. "'Sonne der Gerechtigkeit, gehe auf zu unsrer Zeit . . .' Notizen zur so-
   laren Motivik im Verhältnis von Gott und König." Pp. 188–97 in *Israel in der
   altorientalischen Welt: Gesammelte Studien zur Kultur und Religionsgeschichte
   des antiken Israel.* Edited by Dagmar Pruin and Markus Witte. BZAW 444.
   Berlin: de Gruyter, 2013.

Loretz, Oswald. "Der kanaanäische Ursprung des biblischen Gottesnamens EL
   ŠADDAJ." *UF* 12 (1980) 420–21.

Lucchesi Palli, Elisabeth. "Abraham." *LCI* 1:20–35.

Lührmann, Dieter. "Gerechtigkeit III. Neues Testament." *TRE* 9: 414–20.

Lust, J., E. Eynikel, and K. Hauspie. *A Greek-English Lexicon of the Septuagint.* 2 vols. Stuttgart: Deutsche Bibelgesellschaft, 1992, 1996.

Luther, Martin. *Genesisvorlesung (Kap. 1–17).* WA 42. Weimar: Hermann Böhlaus Nachfolger, 1911.

_____. "Vorrede auff die Weisheit Salomonis." Pp. 1699–1702 in *D. Martin Luther: Die gantze Heilige Schrifft Deudsch Wittenberg 1545. Letzte zu Luthers Lebzeiten erschienene Ausgabe,* vol. 2. Edited by Hans Volz. Munich: Rogner & Bernhard, 1972.

Lutzky, Harriet. "Shadday as a Goddess Epithet." *VT* 48 (1998) 15–36.

MacLaurin, E. C. B. "Shaddai." *AbrN* 3 (1961–1962) 99–118.

Marböck, Johannes. *Gottes Weisheit unter uns: Zur Theologie des Buches Sirach.* HBS 6. Freiburg: Herder, 1995.

_____. *Weisheit im Wandel: Untersuchungen zur Weisheitstheologie bei Ben Sira. Neuauflage mit Nachwort und Bibliographie.* BZAW 272. Berlin: de Gruyter, 1999.

Markschies, Christoph. "Heis Theos—Ein Gott? Der Monotheismus und das antike Christentum." Pp. 209–34 in *Polytheismus und Monotheismus in den Religionen des Vorderen Orients.* Edited by Manfred Krebernik and Jürgen van Oorschot. AOAT 298. Münster: Ugarit, 2002.

Maul, Stefan. "Der assyrische König: Hüter der Weltordnung." Pp. 65–77 in *Gerechtigkeit: Richten und Retten in der abendländischen Tradition und ihren altorientalischen Ursprüngen.* Edited by Jan Assmann, Bernd Janowski, and Michael Welker. Munich: Wilhelm Fink, 1998.

Mehlhausen, Joachim, ed. *Recht—Macht—Gerechtigkeit.* VWGTh 14. Gütersloh: Gütersloher, 1998.

Mettinger, Tryggve N. D. "YAHWEH ZEBAOTH צבאות יהוה." *DDD*[2]: 920–24.

Michaelis, Wilhelm. "κράτος κτλ." *TWNT* 3: 905–14.

Michel, Diethelm. *Begriffsuntersuchung über sädäq-sᵉdaqa und ᵃmät-ᵃmuna.* Unpublished Habilitationsschrift Universität Heidelberg, 1964.

_____. *Grundlegung einer hebräischen Syntax, Teil 1: Sprachwissenschaftliche Methodik, Genus und Numerus des Nomens.* Neukirchen-Vluyn: Neukirchener, 1977.

Moberly, R. W. L. *Old Testament Theology: Reading the Hebrew Bible as Christian Scripture.* Grand Rapids: Baker, 2013.

Montevecchi, Orsolina. "Pantokrator." Pp. 402–23 in *Studi in onore di A. Calderini e R. Paribeni,* vol. 2. Milano: Ceschina, 1957.

Moor, Johannes C. de, and Klaas Spronk. *A Cuneiform Anthology of Religious Texts from Ugarit.* SSS.NS 6. Leiden: Brill, 1987.

Moulton, James Hope, and Goerge Milligan. *The Vocabulary of the Greek Testament Illustrated from the Papyri and Other Non-Literary Sources.* London: Hodder & Stougthon, 1914–1929.

Mulder, Otto. "Two Approaches: Simon the High Priest and YHWH God of Israel / God of All in Sirach 50." Pp. 221–34 in *Ben Sira's God.* Edited by Renate Egger-Wenzel. BZAW 321. Berlin: de Gruyter, 2002.

Müller, Reinhard. "The Origins of Yʜᴡʜ in Light of the Earliest Psalms." Pp. 207–37 in *The Origins of Yahwism.* Edited by Jürgen van Oorschot and Markus Witte. BZAW 484. Berlin: de Gruyter, 2017.

Naveh, Joseph, and Shaul Shaked. *Amulets and Magic Bowls. Aramaic Incantations of Late Antiquity.* Jerusalem: Magnes, 1998.

_____. *Magic Spells and Formulae: Aramaic Incantations of Late Antiquity.* Jerusalem: Magnes, 1993.

Nestler, Julius. *Die Kabbala: Von Papus: Autorisierte Übersetzung.* Leipzig: Altmann, 1910.

Neumann, Mathias. "(El) Šadday: A Plea for an Egyptian Derivation of the God and Its Name." *WO* 46 (2016) 244–63.

Neusner, Jacob. *Messiah in Context: Israel's History and Destiny in Formative Judaism.* Philadelphia: University Press of America, 1988.

Niehr, Herbert. *Der höchste Gott: Alttestamentlicher JHWH-Glaube im Kontext syrisch-kanaanäischer Religion des 1. Jahrtausends v. Chr.* BZAW 190. Berlin: de Gruyter, 1990.

_____. *Herrschen und Richten: Die Wurzel špṭ im Alten Orient und im Alten Testament.* FB 54. Würzburg: Echter, 1986.

_____. *Religionen in Israels Umwelt.* NEchtB Ergänzungsband 5. Stuttgart: Echter, 1998.

_____. "The Constitutive Principles for Establishing Justice and Order in Northwest Semitic Societies with Special Reference to Ancient Israel." *ZABR* 3 (1997) 112–30.

Niehr, Herbert, and Georg Steins. "שַׁדַּי‎ *šaddaj*." *ThWAT* 7:1078–1104.

Nöldeke, Theodor. "Anzeigen: Friedr. Delitzsch, Prolegomena eines neuen hebräisch-aramäischen Wörterbuchs zum Alten Testament, Leipzig 1886." *ZDMG* 40 (1886) 718–43.

Nordheim, Miriam von. *Geboren von der Morgenröte? Psalm 110 in Tradition, Redaktion und Rezeption.* WMANT 117. Neukirchen-Vluyn: Neukirchener, 2008.

Noth, Martin. *Die israelitischen Personennamen im Rahmen der gemeinsemitischen Namengebung.* BWANT III/10. Stuttgart: Kohlhammer, 1928.

Novum Testamentum Graece. Based on the work of Eberhard and Erwin Nestle. Edited by Barbara and Kurt Aland et al. 28th Revised Edition. Edited by the Institute for New Testament Textual Research Münster / Westphalia. Stuttgart: Deutsche Bibelgesellschaft, 2012.

Oates, Whitney J., and Eugene O'Neill, eds. *The Complete Greek Drama: All Extant Tragedies of Aeschylus, Sophocles and Euripides, and the Comedies of Aristophanes and Menander, in a Variety of Translations.* 2 vols. New York: Random House, 1938.

Oberhänsli-Widmer, Gabrielle. *Hiob in jüdischer Antike und Moderne: Die Wirkungsgeschichte Hiobs in der jüdischen Literatur.* Neukirchen-Vluyn: Neukirchener, 2003.

Oegema, Gerbern S. *The Anointed and His People: Messianic Expectations from the Maccabees to Bar Kochba.* JSPSup 27. Sheffield: Sheffield Academic Press, 1998.

Oeming, Manfred. *Biblische Hermeneutik: Eine Einführung.* 3rd ed. Darmstadt: Wissenschaftliche Buchgesellschaft, 2010.

_____. *Gesamtbiblische Theologien der Gegenwart: Das Verhältnis von AT und NT in der hermeneutischen Diskussion seit Gerhard von Rad.* 2nd ed. Stuttgart: Kohlhammer, 1987.

_____. "Salomo-Christologie im Neuen Testament." Pp. 57–76 in *Gegenwart des lebendigen Christus: Festschrift für Michael Welker.* Edited by Günter Thomas and Andreas Schüle. Leipzig: Evangelische Verlagsanstalt, 2007.

Otto, Eckart. *Altorientalische und biblische Rechtsgeschichte: Gesammelte Studien.* BZABR 8. Wiesbaden: Harrassowitz, 2008.

_____. "'Um Gerechtigkeit im Land sichtbar werden zu lassen . . .' Zur Vermittlung von Recht und Gerechtigkeit im Alten Orient, in der Hebräischen Bibel und in der Moderne." Pp. 107–45 in *Recht—Macht—Gerechtigkeit.* Edited by Joachim Mehlhausen. VWGTh 14. Gütersloh: Gütersloher, 1998.

_____. *Theologische Ethik des Alten Testaments.* ThW 3,2. Stuttgart: Kohlhammer, 1994.

Perdue, Leo G. *The Sword and the Stylus: An Introduction to Wisdom in the Age of Empire.* Grand Rapids: Eerdmans, 2008.

Pfeiffer, Henrik. *Jahwes Kommen von Süden: Jdc 5; Hab 3; Dtn 33 und Ps 68 in ihrem literatur- und theologiegeschichtlichem Umfeld.* FRLANT 211. Göttingen: Vandenhoeck & Ruprecht, 2005.

_____. "The Origin of Yhwh and its Attestation." Pp. 115–44 in *The Origins of Yahwism.* Edited by Jürgen van Oorschot and Markus Witte. BZAW 484. Berlin: de Gruyter, 2017.

Pietsch, Michael. *Die Kultreform Josias: Studien zur Religionsgeschichte Israels in der späten Königszeit.* FAT 86. Tübingen: Mohr Siebeck, 2013.

_____. *"Dieser ist der Spross Davids . . .". Studien zur Rezeptionsgeschichte der Nathanverheißung.* WMANT 100. Neukirchen-Vluyn: Neukirchener, 2003.

Plato. "Cratylus." *Plato in Twelve Volumes: Cratylus, Parmenides, Greater Hippias, Lesser Hippias.* Trans. by Harold N. Fowler. LCL 167. Cambridge: Harvard University Press, 1926.

Plöger, Otto. *Theokratie und Eschatologie.* WMANT 2. Neukirchen-Vluyn: Neukirchener, 1959.

Preuß, Horst Dietrich. *Das Alte Testament in christlicher Predigt.* Stuttgart: Kohlhammer, 1984.

Procksch, Otto. *Theologie des Alten Testaments.* Gütersloh: Gütersloher, 1950.

Pury, Albert de. "Wie und wann wurde ›der Gott‹ zu ›Gott‹?." Pp. 121–42 in *Gott nennen: Gottes Namen und Gott als Name.* Edited by Ingolf U. Dalferth and Philipp Stoellger. Religion in Philosophy and Theology 35. Tübingen: Mohr Siebeck, 2008.

Quack, Joachim Friedrich. *Einführung in die altägyptische Literaturgeschichte III. Die demotische und gräko-ägyptische Literatur.* Einführungen und Quellentexte zur Ägyptologie 3. 2nd ed. Münster: LIT, 2009.

Radt, Stefan, ed. *Tragicorum Graecorum Fragmenta*, vol. 3: *Aeschylus.* Göttingen: Vandenhoeck & Ruprecht, 1985.

Rashi. *Raschis Pentateuchkommentar. Vollständig ins Deutsche übertragen und mit einer Einleitung versehen von Rabbiner Dr. Selig Bamberger.* 4th ed. Basel: Victor Goldschmidt, 1994.

Redford, Donald B. *A Study of the Biblical Story of Joseph (Genesis 37–50)*. VTSup 20. Leiden: Brill, 1970.

Reimer, David J. "Old Testament Christology." Pp. 380–400 in *King and Messiah in Israel and the Ancient Near East*. Edited by John Day. JSOTSup 270. Sheffield: Sheffield Academic Press, 1998.

Rendtorff, Rolf. *Theologie des Alten Testaments: Ein kanonischer Entwurf*. 2 vols. Neukirchen-Vluyn: Neukirchener, 1999.2001.

Renz, Johannes, and Walter Röllig. *Handbuch der Althebräischen Epigraphik: Teil 1: Text und Kommentar*. Darmstadt: Wissenschaftliche Buchgesellschaft, 1995.

Reventlow, Henning Graf. *Hauptprobleme der alttestamentlichen Theologie im 20. Jahrhundert*. EdF 173. Darmstadt: Wissenschaftliche Buchgesellschaft, 1982.

_____. *Hauptprobleme der Biblischen Theologie im 20. Jahrhundert*. EdF 203. Darmstadt: Wissenschaftliche Buchgesellschaft, 1983.

Reynolds, Bennie H. "What are Demons of Error? The Meaning of שידי טעתא and Israelite Child Sacrifices." *RdQ* 88 (2007) 593–613.

Robert, C. "El Shaddaï et Jéhova." *Muséon* (1891) 1–15.

Roeder, Günther. *Die ägyptische Götterwelt*. Düsseldorf: Artemis & Winkler, 1998.

_____. *Kulte und Orakel im alten Ägypten*. Düsseldorf: Artemis & Winkler, 1998.

Roscher, Wilhelm Heinrich. *Ausführliches Lexikon der griechischen und römischen Mythologie*, vol. 3/1. Leipzig: Teubner, 1902.

Rose, Martin. *Une herméneutique de l'Ancien Testament: Comprendre—se comprendre—faire comprendre*. MoBi 46. Geneva: Labor et fides, 2003.

Rösel, Christoph. *Die messianische Redaktion des Psalters: Studien zu Entstehung und Theologie der Sammlung Psalm 2–89**. CThM 19. Stuttgart: Calwer, 1999.

Rösel, Martin. *Adonaj—Warum Gott 'Herr' genannt wird*. FAT 29. Tübingen: Mohr Siebeck, 2000.

_____. "Die Übersetzung der Gottesnamen in der Genesis-Septuaginta." Pp. 357–77 in *"Ernten, was man sät." Festschrift für Klaus Koch*. Edited by Dwight R. Daniels, Uwe Gleßmer, and Martin Rösel. Neukirchen-Vluyn: Neukirchener, 1991.

_____. "Theo-Logie der Griechischen Bibel. Zur Wiedergabe der Gottesaussagen im LXX-Pentateuch." *VT* 48 (1998) 49–62.

Rüger, Hans Peter. *Die Weisheitsschrift aus der Kairoer Geniza: Text, Übersetzung und philologischer Kommentar*. Tübingen: Mohr Siebeck, 1991.

Sachs, Nelly. *Gedichte, herausgegeben und mit einem Nachwort versehen von Hilde Domin*. Frankfurt am Main: Suhrkamp, 1977.

Saito, Tadashi. *Die Mosevorstellungen im Neuen Testament*. Europäische Hochschulschriften. Theologie 100. Frankfurt am Main: Peter Lang, 1977.

Saur, Markus. *Die Königspsalmen: Studien zur Entstehung und Theologie*. BZAW 340. Berlin: de Gruyter, 2004.

Scharbert, Josef. "Gerechtigkeit I. Altes Testament." *TRE* 9: 404–11.

Schimanowski, Gottfried. *Weisheit und Messias: Die jüdischen Voraussetzungen der urchristlichen Präexistenzchristologie*. WUNT II/17. Tübingen: Mohr Siebeck, 1985.

Schipper, Bernd U., and D. Andrew Teeter, eds. *Wisdom and Torah: The Reception of 'Torah' in the Wisdom Literature of the Second Temple Period.* JSJSup 163. Leiden: Brill, 2013.

Schleiermacher, Friedrich Daniel Ernst. *Der christliche Glaube nach den Grundsätzen der evangelischen Kirche im Zusammenhange dargestellt.* 2 vols. 3rd ed. Berlin: G. Reimer, 1835.1836.

Schmid, Hans Heinrich. *Gerechtigkeit als Weltordnung: Hintergrund und Geschichte des alttestamentlichen Gerechtigkeitsbegriffes.* BHT 40. Tübingen: Mohr Siebeck, 1968.

Schmid, Konrad. *Erzväter und Exodus: Untersuchungen zur doppelten Begründung der Ursprünge Israels innerhalb der Geschichtsbücher des Alten Testaments.* WMANT 81. Neukirchen-Vluyn: Neukirchener, 1999.

_____. "Herrschererwartungen und -aussagen im Jesajabuch. Überlegungen zu ihrer synchronen Logik und zu ihren diachronen Transformationen." Pp. 175–209 in *The New Things: Eschatology in Old Testament Prophecy; Festschrift for Henk Leene.* Edited by Ferenc Potsma, Klaas Spronk, and Eep Talstra. ACBETSup 3. Maastricht: Shaker, 2002.

Schmitt, Hans-Christoph. *Arbeitsbuch zum Alten Testament: Grundzüge der Geschichte Israels und der alttestamentlichen Schriften.* UTB 2146. 3rd ed. Göttingen: Vandenhoeck & Ruprecht, 2011.

_____. "Der heidnische Mantiker als eschatologischer Jhwhprophet." Pp. 238–54 in *Theologie in Prophetie und Pentateuch: Gesammelte Schriften.* Edited by Ulrike Schorn und Matthias Büttner. BZAW 310. Berlin: de Gruyter, 2001.

_____. "Die Einheit der Schrift und die Mitte des Alten Testaments." Pp. 326–45 in *Theologie in Prophetie und Pentateuch: Gesammelte Schriften.* Edited by Ulrike Schorn and Matthias Büttner. BZAW 310. Berlin: de Gruyter, 2001.

_____. "'Eschatologie' im Enneateuch Gen 1–2 Kön 25. Bedeutung und Funktion der Moselieder Dtn 32,1–43* und Ex 15,1–21*." Pp. 131–49 in *Studien zu Psalmen und Propheten: Festschrift für Hubert Irsigler.* Edited by Carmen Diller. HBS 64. Freiburg: Herder, 2010.

_____. "'Priesterliches' und 'prophetisches' Geschichtsverständnis in der Meerwundererzählung Ex 13,17–14,31." Pp. 203–19 in *Theologie in Prophetie und Pentateuch: Gesammelte Schriften.* Edited by Ulrike Schorn und Matthias Büttner. BZAW 310. Berlin: de Gruyter, 2001.

_____. "Redaktion des Pentateuch im Geiste der Prophetie. Beobachtungen zur Bedeutung der 'Glaubens'-Thematik innerhalb einer Theologie des Pentateuch." Pp. 220–37 in *Theologie in Prophetie und Pentateuch: Gesammelte Schriften.* Edited by Ulrike Schorn und Matthias Büttner. BZAW 310. Berlin: de Gruyter, 2001.

_____. "Tradition der Prophetenbücher in den Schichten der Plagenerzählung Ex 7,1–11,10." Pp. 38–58 in *Theologie in Prophetie und Pentateuch: Gesammelte Schriften.* Edited by Ulrike Schorn and Matthias Büttner. BZAW 310. Berlin: de Gruyter, 2001.

Schreiber, Stefan. *Gesalbter und König: Titel und Konzeptionen der königlichen Gesalbtenerwartung in frühjüdischen und urchristlichen Schriften.* BZNW 105. Berlin: de Gruyter, 2000.

Schröter, Jens, ed. *Jesus Christus, Themen der Theologie 9.* UTB 4213. Tübingen: Mohr Siebeck, 2014.

Schüle, Andreas. *Israels Sohn – Jahwes Prophet: Ein Versuch zum Verhältnis von kanonischer Theologie und Religionsgeschichte anhand der Bileam-Perikope (Num 22–24).* Altes Testament und Moderne 17. Münster: LIT, 2001.

Schwabl, Hans. "Zeus I." *PW* 19: 253–376.

―――. "Zeus II." *PW Suppl.* 15: 994–1481.

Schwarzwäller, Klaus. *Das Alte Testament in Christus.* ThSt 84. Zürich: Theologischer Verlag, 1966.

Schwemer, Daniel. "Das hethitische Reichspantheon: Überlegungen zu Struktur und Genese." Pp. 241–65 in *Götterbilder: Gottesbilder: Weltbilder: Polytheismus und Monotheismus in der Welt der Antike,* vol 1. Edited by Reinhard G. Kratz and Hermann Spieckermann. FAT II/17. 2nd ed. Tübingen: Mohr Siebeck, 2009.

Schwienhorst-Schönberger, Ludger. "Das Hohelied und die Kontextualität des Verstehens." Pp. 81–91 in *Weisheit in Israel.* Edited by David J. A. Clines, Hermann Lichtenberger, and Hans-Peter Müller. Altes Testament und Moderne 12. Münster: LIT, 2003.

Scoralick, Ruth. *Gottes Güte und Gottes Zorn: Die Gottesprädikationen in Ex 34,6f. und ihre intertextuellen Beziehungen zum Zwölfprophetenbuch.* HBS 33. Freiburg: Herder, 2002.

Sedlmeier, Franz. "Ijob und die Auseinandersetzungsliteratur im alten Mesopotamien." Pp. 85–136 in *Das Buch Ijob: Gesamtdeutungen—Einzeltexte—Zentrale Themen.* Edited by Theodor Seidl and Stephanie Ernst. ÖBS 31. Frankfurt am Main: Peter Lang, 2007.

Seebass, Horst. *Genesis II. Vätergeschichte I (11,27–22,24).* Neukirchen-Vluyn: Neukirchener, 1997.

―――. *Genesis III. Josephsgeschichte (37,1–50,26).* Neukirchen-Vluyn: Neukirchener, 2000.

Sencer, Şahin. *Iznik Müzesi: Katalog der antiken Inschriften des Museums von Iznik (Nikaia), II. Inschriften griechischer Städte aus Kleinasien,* vol. 10,1 and 10,2. Bonn: Habelt, 1981.1982.

Septuaginta. Id est Vetus Testamentum graece iuxta LXX interpretes edidit Alfred Rahlfs. Editio altera quam recognovit et emendavit Robert Hanhart. Duo volumina in uno. Stuttgart: Deutsche Bibelgesellschaft, 2006.

Siegfried, Carl, and Bernhard Stade. *Hebräisches Wörterbuch zum Alten Testamente.* Leipzig: Von Veit, 1893.

Sitzler, Dorothea. *"Vorwurf gegen Gott". Ein religiöses Motiv im Alten Orient (Ägypten und Mesopotamien).* StOR 32. Wiesbaden: Harrassowitz, 1995.

Smend, Rudolf. "Schleiermachers Kritik am Alten Testament." Pp. 128–44 in *Epochen der Bibelkritik: Gesammelte Studien 3.* BEvTh 109. Munich: Chr. Kaiser, 1991.

―――. "Theologie im Alten Testament." Pp. 104–17 in *Die Mitte des Alten Testaments: Gesammelte Studien 1.* BEvTh 99. Munich: Chr. Kaiser, 1986.

Smith, Mark S. *The Origins of Biblical Monotheism: Israel's Polytheistic Background and the Ugaritic Texts.* Oxford: Oxford University Press, 2001.

Smith, Ole Langwitz. *Scholia Graeca in Aeschylum quae exstant omnia*, vol. 2.2: *Scholia in septem adversus Thebas continens*. Leipzig: Teubner, 1982.

Sommer, Benjamin D. "Ein neues Modell für Biblische Theologie." Pp. 187–211 in *Theologie und Exegese des Alten Testaments / der Hebräischen Bibel: Zwischenbilanz und Zukunftsperspektiven*. Edited by Bernd Janowski. SBS 200. Stuttgart: Katholisches Bibelwerk, 2005.

Spieckermann, Hermann. "Rechtfertigung I. Altes Testament." *TRE* 28:282–87.

_____. "Recht und Gerechtigkeit im Alten Testament. Politische Wirklichkeit und metaphorischer Anspruch." Pp. 253–73 in *Recht—Macht—Gerechtigkeit*. Edited by Joachim Mehlhausen. VWGTh 14. Gütersloh: Gütersloher, 1998.

Sternberg-el Hotabi, Heike. " 'Die Erde entsteht auf deinen Wink.' Der naturphilosophische Monotheismus des Echnaton." Pp. 45–78 in *Götterbilder: Gottesbilder: Weltbilder: Polytheismus und Monotheismus in der Welt der Antike*, vol. 1. Edited by Reinhard G. Kratz and Hermann Spieckermann. FAT II/17. 2nd ed. Tübingen: Mohr Siebeck, 2009.

Stolz, Fritz. *Psalmen im nachkultischen Raum*. ThSt 129. Zürich: Theologischer Verlag, 1987.

_____. *Strukturen und Figuren im Kult von Jerusalem: Studien zur altorientalischen, vor- und frühisraelitischen Religion*. BZAW 118. Berlin: de Gruyter, 1970.

Strabo. *The Geography*. Literally trans. with notes by Hans Claude Hamilton and W. Falconer. 3 vols. London: Bohn, 1854–57. Repr. London: George Bell & Sons, 1903.

Struppe, Ursula, ed. *Studien zum Messiasbild im Alten Testament*. SBAB 6. Stuttgart: Katholisches Bibelwerk, 1989.

Stuhlmacher, Peter. *Vom Verstehen des Neuen Testaments: Eine Hermeneutik*. GNT 6. 2nd ed. Göttingen: Vandenhoeck & Ruprecht, 1986.

Talmon, Shemaryahu. "Types of Messianic Expectation at the Turn of the Era." Pp. 202–24 in *King, Cult and Calendar in Ancient Israel: Collected Essays*. Leiden: Brill, 1986.

The Soncino Babylonian Talmud, includes Soncino English Text, Talmud Hebrew Aramaic Texts, Rashi Commentary on the Talmud. CD-Rom. www.bnpublishing.com, 2005.

Thesaurus Linguae Graecae ®. A Digital Library of Greek Literature. University of California, Irvine, CA: http://stephanus.tlg.uci.edu/index.php.

Totti, Maria. *Ausgewählte Texte der Isis- und Sarapis-Religion*. SubEpi 12. Hildesheim: Olms, 1985.

Tov, Emanuel. "Three Dimensions of LXX Words." *RB* 83 (1976) 529–44.

Trebilco, Paul. *Jewish Communities in Asia Minor*. SNTSM 69. Cambridge: Cambridge University Press, 1991.

Uehlinger, Christoph. "Arbeit an altorientalischen Gottesnamen: Theonomastik im Spannungsfeld von Sprache, Schrift und Textpragmatik." Pp. 23–71 in *Gott nennen: Gottes Namen und Gott als Name*. Edited by Ingolf U. Dalferth and Philipp Stoellger. Religion in Philosophy and Theology 35. Tübingen: Mohr Siebeck, 2008.

_____. "Das Hiob-Buch im Kontext der altorientalischen Literatur- und Religions-geschichte." Pp. 97–163 in *Das Buch Hiob und seine Interpretationen*. Edited by Thomas Krüger et al. AThANT 88. Zürich: Theologischer Verlag, 2007.

Van der Toorn, Karel. "Anat-Yahu, Some Other Deities and the Jews of Elephantine." *Numen* 39 (1992) 80–101.

Van der Toorn, Karel, and Pieter W. van der Horst, eds., *Dictionary of Deities and Demons in the Bible*. 2nd extensively revised ed. Leiden: Brill, 1999.

Van Oorschot, Jürgen, and Markus Witte, eds. *The Origins of Yahwism*. BZAW 484. Berlin: de Gruyter, 2017.

Van Seters, John. *Prologue to History: The Yahwist as Historian in Genesis*. Zürich: Theologischer Verlag, 1992.

_____. *The Life of Moses: The Yahwist as Historian in Exodus–Numbers*. CBET 10. Kampen: Kok Pharos, 1994.

Vanderlip, V. F. *The Four Greek Hymns of Isidorus and the Cult of Isis*. American Studies in Papyrology 12. Toronto: Hakkert, 1972.

Vielhauer, Roman. *Das Werden des Buches Hosea: Eine redaktionsgeschichtliche Untersuchung*. BZAW 349. Berlin: de Gruyter, 2007.

Vischer, Wilhelm. *Das Christuszeugnis des Alten Testaments*, vols. 1–2/1. 6th ed. Zollikon-Zürich: Evangelischer Verlag, 1943.

_____. *Das Christuszeugnis des Propheten Jeremia: Anhang: Dokumente und Würdigungen zum Fall Vischer 1933*. Bethel 30. Bielefeld: von Bodelschwinghsche Anstalten, 1985.

_____. "Hiob ein Zeuge Jesu Christi." *ZdZ* 5 (1933) 386–414.

Vollenweider, Samuel. "'Der Name, der über jedem anderen Namen ist'. Jesus als Träger des Gottesnamens im Neuen Testament." Pp. 173–86 in *Gott nennen: Gottes Namen und Gott als Name*. Edited by Ingolf U. Dalferth and Philipp Stoellger. Religion in Philosophy and Theology 35. Tübingen: Mohr Siebeck, 2008.

Vorländer, Hermann. *Mein Gott: Die Vorstellungen vom persönlichen Gott im Alten Orient und im Alten Testament*. AOAT 23. Neukirchen-Vluyn: Neukirchener, 1975.

Waschke, Ernst-Joachim. *Der Gesalbte: Studien zur alttestamentlichen Theologie*. BZAW 306. Berlin: de Gruyter, 2001.

Weber, Gregor. *Dichtung und höfische Gesellschaft: Die Rezeption von Zeitgeschichte am Hof der ersten drei Ptolemäer*. Hermes. E 62. Stuttgart: Steiner, 1983.

Weigold, Matthias. "Noah in the Praise of the Fathers: The Flood Story *in nuce*." Pp. 229–44 in *Studies in the Book of Ben Sira*. Edited by Geza G. Xeravits and Jószef Zsengellér. JSJSup 127. Leiden: Brill, 2008.

Weinberg, Joel. "Job versus Abraham. The Quest for the Perfect God-Fearer in Rabbinic Tradition." Pp. 281–96 in *The Book of Job*. Edited by W. A. M. Beuken. BEThL 64. Leuven: Peeters, 1994.

Weippert, Manfred. "Erwägungen zur Etymologie des Gottesnamens ʾĒl Šadday." *ZDMG* 111 (1961) 42–62.

_____. "שַׁדַּי Šaddaj (Gottesname)." *THAT* 2: 873–81.

Wellhausen, Julius. *Die kleinen Propheten übersetzt und erklärt*. 3rd ed. Berlin: Reimer, 1898.

Wengst, Klaus. *Didache (Apostellehre), Barnabasbrief, Zweiter Klemensbrief, Schrift an Diognet: Schriften des Urchristentums 2.* Darmstadt: Wissenschaftliche Buchgesellschaft, 1984.

Westermann, Claus, ed. *Probleme alttestamentlicher Hermeneutik: Aufsätze zum Verstehen des Alten Testaments.* TB 11. Munich: Chr. Kaiser, 1960.

Wicke-Reuter, Ursel. *Göttliche Providenz und menschliche Verantwortung bei Ben Sira und in der frühen Stoa.* BZAW 298. Berlin: de Gruyter, 2000.

Wifall, Walter. "El Shaddai or El of the Fields." *ZAW* 92 (1980) 24–32.

Williamson, H. G. M. *He Has Shown You What is Good: Old Testament Justice Then and Now; The Trinity Lectures, Singapore, 2011.* Cambridge: Lutterworth, 2012.

Winston, David. "Theodicy in the Wisdom of Solomon." Pp. 525–45 in *Theodicy in the World of the Bible.* Edited by Antti Laato and Johannes C. de Moor. Leiden: Brill, 2003.

Wischmeyer, Odo, ed. *Lexikon der Bibelhermeneutik: Begriffe—Methoden—Theorien—Konzepte.* Berlin: de Gruyter, 2009.

Witte, Markus. " 'Aber Gott wird meine Seele erlösen' "—Tod und Leben nach Psalm xlix." Pp. 67–93 in *Von Ewigkeit zu Ewigkeit: Weisheit und Geschichte in den Psalmen.* BThSt 146. Neukirchen-Vluyn: Neukirchener, 2014.

———. " 'Das Gesetz des Lebens' (Sirach 17,11)." Pp. 109–21 in *Texte und Kontexte des Sirachbuchs: Gesammelte Studien zu Ben Sira und zur frühjüdischen Weisheit.* FAT 98. Tübingen: Mohr Siebeck, 2015.

———. "Der Glaube an den einen Gott in der israelitisch-jüdischen Weisheit." Pp. 245–62 in *Texte und Kontexte des Sirachbuchs: Gesammelte Studien zu Ben Sira und zur frühjüdischen Weisheit.* FAT 98. Tübingen: Mohr Siebeck, 2015.

———. "Der Segen Bileams—eine redaktionsgeschichtliche Problemanzeige zum "Jahwisten" in Num 22–24." Pp. 191–213 in *Abschied vom Jahwisten: Die Komposition des Hexateuch in der jüngsten Diskussion.* Edited by Jan Christian Gertz, Konrad Schmid, and Markus Witte. BZAW 315. Berlin: de Gruyter, 2002.

———. *Die biblische Urgeschichte: Redaktions- und theologiegeschichtliche Beobachtungen zu Genesis 1,1–11,26.* BZAW 265. Berlin: de Gruyter, 1998.

———. "Does the Torah Keep Its Promise? Job's Critical Intertextual Dialogue with Deuteronomy." Pp. 54–65 in *Reading Job Intertextually.* Edited by Katherine Dell and Will Kynes. LHBOTS 574. New York: Bloomsbury, 2013.

———. "Hiob und die Väter Israels. Beobachtungen zum Hiobtargum." Pp. 39–61 in *Hiobs Gestalten: Interdisziplinäre Studien zum Bild Hiobs in Judentum und Christentum.* Edited by Markus Witte. SKI NF 2. Leipzig: Evangelische Verlagsanstalt, 2012.

———. *Jesus Christus im Alten Testament: Eine biblisch-theologische Skizze.* SEThV 4. Münster: LIT, 2013.

———. "Job in Conversation with the Torah." Pp. 81–100 in *Wisdom and Torah: The Reception of 'Torah' in the Wisdom Literature of the Second Temple Period.* Edited by Bernd U. Schipper and D. Andrew Teeter. JSJSup 163. Leiden: Brill, 2013.

_____. "Orakel und Gebete im Buch Habakuk." Pp. 67–91 in *Orakel und Gebete: Interdisziplinäre Studien zur Sprache der Religion in Ägypten, Vorderasien und Griechenland in hellenistischer Zeit*. Edited by Johannes F. Diehl and Markus Witte. FAT II/38. Tübingen: Mohr Siebeck, 2009.

_____. *Vom Leiden zur Lehre: Der dritte Redegang (Hiob 21—27) und die Redaktionsgeschichte des Hiobbuches*. BZAW 230. Berlin: de Gruyter, 1994.

_____. "Worship and Holy Places in the Wisdom of Solomon." Pp. 289–303 in *Various Aspects of Worship in Deuterocanonical and Cognate Literature*. Edited by Ibolya Balla, Geza G. Xeravits, and Jószef Zsengellér. DCLY 2016/2017. Berlin: de Gruyter, 2017.

_____, ed. *Gerechtigkeit: Themen der Theologie 6*. UTB 3662. Tübingen: Mohr Siebeck, 2012.

Yonge, Charles Duke. *The Works of Philo: Complete and Unabridged: New Updated Edition*. 8th ed. Peabody, MA: Hendrickson, 2006.

The Yorck Project. *Die Bibel in der Kunst*. Berlin: The Yorck Project. Gesellschaft für Bildarchivierung, 2004, DVD.

Zangenberg, Jürgen K. "The Sanctuary on Mount Gerizim." Pp. 399–418 in *Temple Building and Temple Cult: Architecture and Cultic Paraphernalia of Temples in the Levant (2.–1. Mill. BCE)*. Edited by Jens Kamlah and Henrike Michelau. ADPV 41. Wiesbaden: Harrassowitz, 2012.

Zeller, Dieter. "Κυριος κύριος" *DDD*²: 492–97.

Zenger, Erich. "Was sind Essentials eines theologischen Kommentars zum Alten Testament?" Pp. 213–38 in *Theologie und Exegese des Alten Testaments / der Hebräischen Bibel: Zwischenbilanz und Zukunftsperspektive*. Edited by Bernd Janowski. SBS 200. Stuttgart: Katholisches Bibelwerk, 2005.

Ziemer, Benjamin. *Abram—Abraham: Kompositionsgeschichtliche Untersuchungen zu Genesis 14, 15 und 17*. BZAW 350. Berlin: de Gruyter, 2005.

Zimmerli, Walter. *Grundriß der alttestamentlichen Theologie*. ThW 3,1. 7th ed. Stuttgart: Kohlhammer, 1999.

Zimmermann, Christiane. *Die Namen des Vaters: Studien zu ausgewählten neutestamentlichen Gottesbezeichnungen vor ihrem frühjüdischen und paganen Hintergrund*. AJEC (AGJU) 69. Leiden: Brill, 2007.

Zimmermann, Johannes. *Messianische Texte aus Qumran: Königliche, priesterliche und prophetische Messiasvorstellungen in den Schriftfunden von Qumran*. WUNT II/104. Tübingen: Mohr Siebeck, 1998.

Zimmern, Heinrich, and Hugo Winckler. *Die Keilinschriften und das Alte Testament*. 3rd ed. Berlin: Reuther & Reichard, 1903.

Zorell, Franciscus. *Lexicon Hebraicum et Aramaicum Veteris Testamenti*. Rome: Pontificium Institutum Biblicum, 1954.

Index of Authors

Index of Scripture

Old Testament

128

New Testament

Deuterocanonical Works

Pseudepigrapha

3 Baruch
  1:3   22
  11:9   21

1 Enoch
  6–9   84
  37–71   96
  42   73
  46:1–6   58
  48:2   96
  48:10   96
  52:4   96

4 Ezra
  7:28–29   96
  13:3–4   58

Epistle of Aristeas
  185.2   22, 23

Jubilees
  5:1–20   84
  17:15–18   84

Odes of Solomon
  14:11   21

Psalms of Solomon
  3:8   89
  9:5   47
  10:3–4   35
  14:2   35
  17   95
  17:36   89, 95
  18   95

Sibylline Oracles
  1:66   22
  1:216   21

Sibylline Oracles (cont.)
  2:220   22
  2:222   21
  2:330   22
  2:284   21
  4:51   21
  4:135   21
  8:66   21
  8:82   22
  8:265   22
  11:8   22

Testament of Abraham
  2:3   21
  8:3   22
  15:12   22
  17:11   21

Index of Subjects, Names, Words, and Other Ancient Sources

Subjects and Names